Labor, Nature, and
the Evolution of Humanity

LABOR, NATURE
and the
EVOLUTION *of* HUMANITY

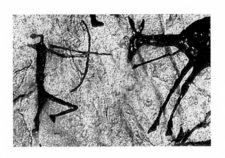

The long view of history

FREDERICK ENGELS
KARL MARX
GEORGE NOVACK
MARY-ALICE WATERS

PATHFINDER
NEW YORK   LONDON   MONTREAL   SYDNEY

Edited by Mary-Alice Waters

ISBN 978-1-60488-120-2
Library of Congress Control Number 2021930993
Manufactured in Canada

COVER DESIGN: Toni Gorton

COVER ILLUSTRATION: Stone Age hunters pursuing deer with bow and
arrow, among the first tools that allowed humans to capture and
consume large, fast animals. Painted around 7000 BC, Los Caballos
Cave in eastern Spain.

Pathfinder
www.pathfinderpress.com
E-mail: pathfinder@pathfinderpress.com

ALSO BY THE AUTHORS

FREDERICK ENGELS
The Condition of the Working Class in England
The Communist Manifesto *(with Marx)*
The Housing Question
Socialism: Utopian and Scientific
The Origin of the Family, Private Property, and the State
Anti-Dühring
Ludwig Feuerbach and the End of Classical German Philosophy
Dialectics of Nature

GEORGE NOVACK
Understanding History
Genocide against the Indians
America's Revolutionary Heritage
Democracy and Revolution
Revolutionary Dynamics of Women's Liberation
An Introduction to the Logic of Marxism
Pragmatism versus Marxism

KARL MARX
Theses on Feuerbach
Communist Manifesto (*with Engels*)
Wage Labor and Capital
The Eighteenth Brumaire of Louis Bonaparte
Contribution to a Critique of Political Economy
Wages, Price, and Profit
The Civil War in the United States (*with Engels*)
Capital
The Civil War in France
Critique of the Gotha Program

Continued on next page

MARY-ALICE WATERS

Is Socialist Revolution in the US Possible?
Cosmetics, Fashions, and the Exploitation of Women
In Defense of the US Working Class
Cuba and the Coming American Revolution
Che's Proletarian Legacy and Cuba's Rectification Process
Thomas Sankara Speaks
Feminism and the Marxist Movement

CONTENTS

Text boxes and illustrations (next page)

TEXT BOXES

ILLUSTRATIONS

FREDERICK ENGELS (1820–1895) was the founding leader, along with Karl Marx, of the modern revolutionary workers movement. Together with Marx, he was the greatest teacher of materialist dialectics.

Engels (right) and Marx review paper they produced during 1848 revolution.

Recruited by tested proletarian leaders to a working-class organization in 1847, Marx and Engels drafted its program, the Communist Manifesto, and took part in forming the Communist League (1847–52). Recalling many years later his first encounters with the workers who won the two young revolutionaries to the League, Engels wrote: "These were the first revolutionary proletarians whom I met, and however far apart our views were at that time—for I still owned, as against their narrow-minded egalitarian Communism a goodly dose of just as narrow-minded philosophical arrogance—I shall never forget the deep impression that these three real men made upon me, who was then still only wanting to become a man."

Marx and Engels led the proletarian wing of the 1848–49 revolution in Germany during which Engels saw

5

combat in the 1849 uprisings in Elberfeld, Baden, and the Palatinate. After the revolution's defeat, he and Marx found refuge in England, where Engels's father owned a textile factory that enabled Engels to support himself and help sustain Marx's growing family as they led the regroupment of the international revolutionary working-class vanguard.

Together they were central leaders of the International Working Men's Association, sometimes called the First International, launched in 1864. They were active in labor struggles in Britain and championed revolutionary struggles around the world, from the Irish and Polish independence movements to the war against the slavocracy in the United States and the 1871 Paris Commune, the world's first working-class government. They followed with keen interest and understanding the diverse fields of scientific investigation exploding during their lifetimes.

After the death of Marx in 1883, Engels led the revolutionary wing of the Second International, founded in 1880, until his own death in 1895. He waged political battles to defend a proletarian course in face of reformist and anarchist currents seeking to divert the working-class movement from the revolutionary course Marx and Engels defended throughout their lives.

After Marx completed the first volume of *Capital* in 1867, Engels promoted the book's circulation internationally. Following Marx's death, he edited Marx's unfinished manuscripts and notes for the second and third volumes of *Capital,* as he continued to collaborate closely with fellow communists across Europe and the United States.

The lifetime example and extensive writings by Marx and Engels have provided the political foundation for the course of proletarian revolutionists and parties worldwide for more than a century and a half.

GEORGE NOVACK (1905–1992) joined the communist movement in the United States in 1933. He remained a member and leader of the Socialist Workers Party until his death, serving for more than thirty years on the party's National Committee.

A student at Harvard in the 1920s, he was deeply affected in the early thirties by Hitler's ascent to power in Germany. That blow to the working class, he came to understand, was the consequence of the Stalinist-led Communist International's refusal to call for united action with the Social Democratic Party to defeat the rising Nazi threat. Under the impact of those events, Novack broke politically from the largely Jewish milieu of writer and artist Communist Party fellow-travelers he had been part of, around the magazine *Menorah Journal,* and joined the Communist League of America, predecessor of the SWP.

Known for his extensive writings on Marxism and the history of philosophy, Novack over his six decades of revolutionary activity shouldered diverse responsibilities as a party leader. He helped lead numerous workers movement defense campaigns, becoming a popular fund-raiser for the SWP and other working-class activity. During World War II he joined the party's industrial trade union fraction as a machinist in Detroit's Hudson auto factory.

As national secretary of the American Committee for the Defense of Leon Trotsky, Novack helped organize the 1937 International Commission of Inquiry, headed by noted US educator John Dewey, which exposed the infamous

1936–38 Moscow frame-up trials. The commission's report dealt a powerful blow to the counterrevolutionary course of the regime headed by Joseph Stalin. The "trials" led to the murder and imprisonment of millions in the Soviet Union and beyond. With the 1940 assassination of Trotsky by Stalin's murder machine, every member of the Political Bureau of the Lenin-led Bolshevik Party at the time of the October 1917 revolution in Russia had been purged, except Stalin himself.

During World War II Novack served as national secretary of the Civil Rights Defense Committee, which won broad support among trade unionists and civil libertarians for eighteen leaders of the Socialist Workers Party and of the Midwest Teamsters strikes and organizing drives. Singled out by the Roosevelt administration for organizing working-class opposition to US imperialism's war aims, they were framed, convicted, and jailed on federal "subversion" charges under the Smith Act, which made it illegal "to teach, advocate and encourage" communist ideas.

Novack helped lead several other civil liberties and political rights battles over the decades, including the landmark federal lawsuit against FBI spying and disruption won by the Socialist Workers Party in 1986.

He was an active participant in the mass struggles from the 1950s through the '70s that brought down Jim Crow segregation. A champion of the rise of the women's liberation movement, he was also active in defense of the Cuban Revolution and in building the powerful movement to end Washington's war against the Vietnamese people.

Novack wrote and spoke widely in defense of Marxism and the communist movement at universities and public forums across the United States and internationally, helping to educate new generations of revolutionists joining the proletarian party that he dedicated his life to building.

KARL MARX (1818–1883)

Marx with his daughter Jenny in London, 1864.

No more perceptive summary of the life of Marx exists than the words of his closest comrade in arms, Frederick Engels, spoken at the graveside in London on March 17, 1883, three days after Marx died.

On the 14th of March, at a quarter to three in the afternoon, the greatest living thinker ceased to think. He had been left alone for scarcely two minutes, and when we came back we found him in his armchair, peacefully gone to sleep—but forever.

An immeasurable loss has been sustained both by the militant proletariat of Europe and America, and by historical science, in the death of this man. The gap that has been left by the departure of this mighty spirit will soon enough make itself felt.

Just as Darwin discovered the law of development of organic nature, so Marx discovered the law of development of human history: the simple fact, hitherto concealed by an overgrowth of ideology, that mankind must first of all eat, drink, have shelter and clothing, before it can pursue politics, science, art, religion, etc. That therefore, the production of the immediate material means of subsistence and consequently the degree of economic development attained by a given people or during a given epoch form the foundation upon which the state institutions, the legal conceptions, art, and even the ideas on religion, of the people concerned have been evolved, and in the light of which they must, therefore, be explained, instead of vice versa, as had hitherto been the case.

But that is not all. Marx also discovered the special law of motion governing the present-day capitalist mode of production and the bourgeois society that this mode of production has created. The discovery of surplus value suddenly threw light on the problem, in trying to solve which all previous investigations, of both bourgeois economists and socialist critics, had been groping in the dark.

Two such discoveries would be enough for one lifetime. Happy the man to whom it is granted to make even one such discovery. But in every single field which Marx investigated—and he investigated very many fields, none of them superficially—in every field, even in that of mathematics, he made independent discoveries.

Such was the man of science. But this was not even half the man. Science was for Marx a historically dynamic, revolutionary force. However great the joy with which he welcomed a new discovery in some theoretical science whose practical application perhaps it was as yet quite impossible to envisage, he experienced quite another kind of joy when the discovery involved immediate revolutionary changes in industry and in historical development in general. For example, he followed closely the development of the discoveries made in the field of electricity and recently those of Marcel Deprez.

For Marx was before all else a revolutionist. His real mission in life was to contribute, in one way or another, to the overthrow of capitalist society and of the state institutions which it had brought into being, to contribute to the liberation of the modern proletariat, which he was the first to make conscious of its own position and its needs, conscious of the conditions of its emancipation. Fighting was his element. And he fought with a passion, a tenacity and a success such as few could rival.

His work on the first *Rheinische Zeitung* (1842), the Paris *Vorwärts!* (1844), *Deutsche-Brüsseler Zeitung* (1847), the *Neue Rheinische Zeitung* (1848–49), the *New York Tribune* (1852–61), and in addition to these a host of militant pamphlets, work in organizations in Paris, Brussels, and London, and finally, crowning all, the formation of the great International Working Men's Association—this was indeed an achievement of which its founder might well have been proud even if he had done nothing else.

And, consequently, Marx was the best-hated and most calumniated man of his time. Governments, both absolutist and republican, deported him from their territories. Bourgeois, whether conservative or ultra-democratic, vied with one another in heaping slanders upon him. All this he brushed aside as though it were cobweb, ignoring it, answering only when extreme necessity compelled him.

And he died beloved, revered and mourned by millions of revolutionary fellow-workers—from the mines of Siberia to California, in all parts of Europe and America—and I make bold to say that though he may have had many opponents he had hardly one personal enemy.

His name will endure through the ages, and so also will his work!

MARY-ALICE WATERS
is a longtime leader of the
Socialist Workers Party
and president of Pathfinder
Press.

Waters was won to rev-
olutionary working-class
politics in the early 1960s
by the response of the Socialist Workers Party to the
deepening class battles unfolding in the US and internationally. While in college, she participated in the mass
sit-ins and other actions that were part of bringing down
Jim Crow race segregation. As the working people of Cuba,
under the leadership of Fidel Castro and the Rebel Army,
advanced the first socialist revolution in the Americas and
defeated the mercenary invasion organized by Washington at the Bay of Pigs, she joined with other students at
Carleton College in building what was for a time the largest campus chapter of the Fair Play for Cuba Committee.

Her commitment to communist politics deepened during a year of study in France in 1961–62 that coincided
with the final months of the Algerian independence struggle. Waters took part in the massive Paris demonstrations
supporting the Algerian people. She experienced firsthand
the fascist violence of cops in the hated "security" corps
(CRS) backing ultrarightist military officers who in 1961
formed the Secret Army Organization (OAS), seeking to
overturn the French government and preserve colonial
rule of Algeria. On returning to the US, Waters joined
the Young Socialist Alliance in 1962 and Socialist Workers
Party in 1964.

Among many party responsibilities since then, Waters
has edited several publications presenting the party's po-

litical positions and been central to leading the SWP's international work, especially its activity in defense of the Cuban Revolution. In the 1980s she led three sessions of the party's leadership school focused on political writings by Marx and Engels. From the late 1960s to today, Waters has shouldered central responsibility for leading the party's fight for women's liberation, without which no revolutionary workers movement can be built. She speaks widely in the US and abroad on these and other aspects of communist politics.

Waters was national secretary and then chairperson (1967–68) of the Young Socialist Alliance. She has been a member of the SWP National Committee since 1967. Waters traveled to France in 1968 to cover the student-labor uprising for the *Militant* newsweekly, as well as to Montreal in 1970 to report for the paper on resistance to Ottawa's imposition of the War Measures Act on Quebec. She edited the *Militant* from 1969 through the early 1970s and has been president of Pathfinder Press since 1992. In addition to editing more than thirty books on the Cuban Revolution, she is the author, editor, or major contributor to many other works published by Pathfinder Press and *New International* magazine.

Without materialist dialectics, there can be no working-class revolution

Mary-Alice Waters

Labor, next to the materials from nature it transforms, is the source of all wealth. But it is infinitely more. It's the basic condition for all human existence, and this to such an extent we have to say that labor created man himself.

FREDERICK ENGELS, 1876

This is a book about where humanity came from and how we arrived where we are today.

Why is that important?

Quite simply, because without an understanding of the dawn of humanity and our subsequent evolution—with its contradictions and ensuing dialectical leaps, its unanticipated combinations and inevitable unevennesses—working people the world over are doomed to remain prisoners of the moment in which we live. Prisoners of the capitalist epoch, unable to see beyond the relations of class exploitation that warp every aspect of our lives, ideas, social relations, and even personal values.

The dog-eat-dog world of capitalism, however, is not eternal. Nor is it the product of "human nature," as we are often told.

Class-divided societies, of which capitalism is but the most recent stage, arose only *a few thousand* years ago. That's not even a blink of the eye in the history of humanity. Those class divisions emerged along with the increasingly productive social labor of our ancestors, which enabled them to produce more than needed for mere survival. Along with that surplus, however, arose private property, priesthoods, and states, together with their armies and other repressive institutions used to defend the property, power, and privileges of the ruling few.

For its part, the social and political dictatorship of capital is barely *a few hundred* years old. Based on work for wages by the great majority of us who have no property to live off and must sell our ability to labor to an employer, capitalism too had a beginning under particular historical conditions. It will have an end under others.

Armed with this long view of history, a working-class vanguard of all nationalities, religions, skin colors, and both sexes—engaged in struggles together with millions of other working people—can develop the experience, political confidence, and fighting capacities to chart a revolutionary course. A course that can take state power out of the hands of the propertied rulers and build governing institutions created by the working class. Only then will a society worth living in for the great majority, one free of class exploitation and oppression, become possible.

All this is contrary to everything we are taught—and not taught—whether in school or factory, prison or place of worship.

For the owners of capital, this is dangerous knowledge. For the working class, to whom this dangerous knowledge belongs, it opens a window on the road forward to a different and better world.

~

Labor, Nature, and the Evolution of Humanity brings together a number of writings by revolutionary leaders of the working class from the middle of the nineteenth century to today.

The book includes "The Part Played by Labor in the Transition from Ape to Man" by Frederick Engels, who along with Karl Marx made up the founding leadership of the modern working-class movement. Engels's unfinished text drew on the groundbreaking discoveries of Charles Darwin and other nineteenth-century pioneers in what was then the young science of evolutionary biology. First published in German in 1896, a year after Engels's death, this short piece appeared in English translation only in 1934.

In it Engels explains the place of labor, the "basic condition for all human existence," in transforming nature and ourselves, creating the conditions out of which human society is born. He explains the centrality of the evolution of the human hand with its opposable thumb and resulting facility in making and using tools. From that beginning, speech, the enlarging human brain, and other attributes distinguishing us from the rest of the animal world have evolved.

It is the history of human *social relations*, however, that Engels focuses on above all, relations developed over millennia as our productive capacities expanded. "The animal merely *uses* its environment," Engels writes. "Man by his changes makes it serve his ends, *masters* it," and passes along knowledge and new skills from one generation to the next. "This is the final, essential distinction between man and other animals, and once again it is labor that brings this about."

In explaining this interconnection of social labor and nature, Engels built on the materialist foundations laid by Marx. Capitalism expands production only "by simultaneously undermining the original sources of all wealth— the soil and the worker," *nature and labor,* as Marx wrote in *Capital.* Beginning with the simplest elements of capitalism—the individual commodity and wage-labor, which were leading to the modern factory system of production and trade—Marx went on to demonstrate why only the working-class conquest of power can preserve not just life and limb but an earth, skies, and waters compatible with human development.

Similarly, in the article included here Engels explains, "Let us not, however, flatter ourselves overmuch on account of our human victories over nature. For each such victory nature takes its revenge on us. Each victory, it is true, in the first place brings about results we expected, but in the second and third places it has quite different, unforeseen effects which only too often cancel the first consequences." And always qualify them.

Engels cited the example of European maritime exploration and colonial conquest, one of the earliest sources of capital accumulation. When Christopher Columbus landed in the Americas, Engels wrote, "he did not know that by doing so he was giving a new lease on life to slavery, which in Europe had long ago been done away with, and laying the basis for the Negro slave trade." Nor did Spanish planters in Cuba care that their slash-and-burn deforestation, aimed at turning a quick profit on coffee beans, would wash away topsoil for generations to come.

"We are gradually learning to get a clear view of the indirect, more remote social effects of our production activity," Engels wrote, "and so are afforded an opportunity to control and regulate these effects as well. This regulation, however, requires something more than mere knowledge.

"It requires a complete revolution in our hitherto existing mode of production, and simultaneously a revolution in our whole contemporary social order."

Engels, like Marx and other working-class leaders cited in these pages, didn't celebrate knowledge for the sake of knowledge. They were students of science and history, above all, because that knowledge was necessary to organize the working class and its allies and help them find the road to emancipation.

~

The articles by George Novack, a decades-long leader of the Socialist Workers Party in the US, are taken from *The Long View of History*. First published in 1960 by the predecessor of Pathfinder Press and kept in print ever since, that small book has served to educate several political generations of revolutionary-minded youth in the foundations of scientific socialism. I count myself among them.

"How Humanity Climbed to Civilization" and "The Main Course of American History" began in 1955 as classes taught by Novack to members and new young recruits to the Socialist Workers Party at a summer school and camp organized by the Los Angeles branch of the party. It was a time of growing political awakening. As is the case today, the youth being attracted to the communist movement knew nothing of the scientific foundations of Marxism.

Novack's small book, as he explained in a foreword to the first edition, was directed toward "newly awakened minds," offering "a popularized account of the main line of evolution from fish to mankind," and from the origins of human society "to contemporary capitalism in the United States." It is, he insisted, "an extremely simplified outline of the immense and complex range" of that process. Some dates and other facts concerning humanity's prehistory cited by Novack and Engels have been altered by scientific discoveries over the decades. More recent findings, however, have only confirmed the fundamental course of humanity's social development the authors present.

The 1955 classes, Novack explains, were "aimed against two prevailing notions" upholding "the sanctity of the existing system." One is that it is "impossible, undesirable, or somehow unscientific to seek out the central course of development in history, above all in the history of society; to link together its successive stages and place them in proper sequence; to distinguish the lower form from the higher; and indicate the nature of the next steps."

The second prejudice, Novack said, is the assumption that the capitalist regime in the United States "embodies the highest attainable mode of life and an unsurpassable type of social organization." Both propositions are "wrong in theory and thoroughly reactionary in their practical consequences," he said. As against them, he hoped to explain why aspirations among working people "for a better way of life are reasonable and realistic. They are consistent with sound scientific premises."

The pages to come include illustrations and photographs to aid readers in following what Novack calls "the main line of human progress" described in *Labor, Nature, and the Evolution of Humanity*. Throughout the two 1955 classes, we have added supplementary text boxes with brief excerpts from historical and political writings by Marx, Engels, and Novack, as well as by revolutionary working-class leaders

Farrell Dobbs, Evelyn Reed, Leon Trotsky, Armando Hart, and Jack Barnes.

The time when Novack's talks were given is also important to note. September 1955 was barely ten years after the end of the most massive interimperialist slaughter in history. The memory of the intertwined class and national conflicts subsumed within what is called World War II—as well as the consequences still unfolding—weighed heavily in all politics, in North America and worldwide.

In the United States, the more than year-long Montgomery bus boycott, which began in December 1955, was only a few months away. It was to be the first great battle of the powerful proletarian-led mass movement by African Americans that brought down the apartheid-like system of race segregation in the South. That historic movement changed forever the prospects in the US for broad and united working-class leadership and solidarity.

The merger of the two largest and strongest national trade union federations—the American Federation of Labor (AFL), and the Congress of Industrial Organizations (CIO)—which took place in 1955 was being hailed by many in the working class and labor movement as a powerful step forward. In fact, it was soon shown to be another manifestation of the decades-long retreat of the labor movement's misleaderships and their willing subordination of the unions to the electoral aspirations of the Democratic Party and to the bosses' two-party system.

On the world stage, the momentous colonial independence battles in India, Indonesia, and China, accelerated by World War II, had been victorious. Only two years earlier, the US-led war aimed at defeating the independence and unification of Korea had been fought to a standstill by the Korean people and their Chinese allies, ending in the north-south partition of that nation and an uneasy truce; US troops and weaponry remain stationed on sovereign Korean soil to this day. The French colonizers had been driven out of Vietnam in 1954, only to be replaced by US imperialism and its puppet regimes in the southern half of the country.

Egypt's Suez Canal was still firmly under the control of British and French imperialism, and a 1953 coup in Iran engineered by Washington and London had overthrown the short-lived popularly elected government of Mohammad Mossadegh and reimposed the pro-imperialist Persian monarchy.

The triumph of the Cuban Revolution, the first and so far only socialist revolution in the Americas—and with it the beginning of the renewal of communist leadership internationally—was still almost half a decade away.

The sweep of anticolonial struggles across Africa and the Caribbean was also still to come, both drawing strength from and further emboldening the Black rights movement in the US.

In February 1956 came the speech by prime minister Nikita Khrushchev to a closed session of the Twentieth Congress of the Communist Party of the Soviet Union, acknowledging the enormity of the crimes of the Stalin-led bureaucratic caste, until then totally denied. Popular uprisings by workers and youth against the oppressive course of the Stalinist regimes in Hungary and Poland later that year further accelerated the disintegration and deepening contradictions of world Stalinism, with broad international repercussions.

Thinking about even a few of these historic events that shaped the US and world class struggle shortly before or after Novack first gave these classes helps readers better understand the sweep of natural and human history he was in the midst of describing.

~

Such an understanding of history is important in face of today's spreading "cancel culture" among privileged middle-class layers in the universities, foundations, media and government circles, as well as the profoundly anti-working-class, anti-science "woke" politics they promote. The reactionary use of "social media" as a weapon to try to silence and destroy the lives and livelihoods of anyone who expresses disagreement with ideas promoted by these comfortable layers has become commonplace.

Schools and universities have become seedbeds of censorship where young people are supposed to be guaranteed "safe spaces" and "protected" from words, ideas, facts, or artistic works deemed by the wise to be literally "hurtful" or "offensive" to the youth. Far from being challenged to expand historical and cultural horizons—to always be "broadening your scope," as Malcolm X urged workers and youth—students are being taught that great works of art, literature, and scientific conquests of past generations, from which we learn and which we transform as we build on today, are at best irrelevant, if not products of "white supremacy," "toxic masculinity," "transphobia," and "misogyny."

Classics of literature—from Homer to Mark Twain's *Huckleberry Finn*, from Shakespeare to *Pride and Prejudice* by Jane Austen, Harper Lee's *To Kill a Mockingbird*, and much more—have been labeled "racist" and sometimes withdrawn from classrooms and even high school libraries. The historically Black college Howard University has dissolved its classics department to "prioritize" other subjects. Brandeis University has issued an "Oppressive

Language List," which includes the words "he/she" because they "lump all people under masculine language or within the gender binary" of either male or female. It includes the term "picnic" because some might associate the word with photos they may have seen of crowds at Jim Crow–era lynchings of African Americans and be "injured" by it.

Public figures like J.K. Rowling, author of the widely read Harry Potter books, who publicly defend the conquests of the fight for women's liberation and speak the scientific truth that there are two sexes with distinct biological characteristics, become targets of social media mob assaults for being "transphobic." Publishing contracts and speaking engagements are canceled, as some libraries and bookstores withdraw their works from the shelves.

Charles Darwin, the pioneer of evolutionary biology and one of the most outstanding scientists of the nineteenth century, has now joined the long line of targets.

The year 2021 marked the hundred-fiftieth anniversary of the publication of Darwin's ground-breaking work *The Descent of Man, and Selection in Relation to Sex*. The book was considered scandalous at the time. Darwin became the target of a nineteenth-century "cancel" campaign (meager by today's social media standards) because he applied to human origins the understanding of evolutionary biology developed in his *Origin of Species*, published more than a decade earlier.

Darwin refuted the views of many prominent scientists of his day, such as Harvard professor Louis Agassiz, a favorite of the Southern slavocracy, who contended there are eight human species, and each had its own separate divine creation. Darwin's work effectively established that human beings are not the product of a heavenly or otherwise special creation but evolved through natural selection from a single common origin among the primates millions of years ago. He demonstrated that *all* humans are a *single* species and that the differences between humans and other animals, especially the higher primates, are "of degree and not of kind."

Darwin and the science of evolutionary biology he founded have been a target of reactionary and obscurantist forces in the capitalist world for more than a hundred sixty years. One infamous example was the 1925 "Monkey Trial" in which high school teacher John T. Scopes of Dayton, Tennessee, who taught his students Darwin's evolutionary findings, was convicted of violating a state law that barred the teaching of "any theory that denies the story of the Divine Creation of man as taught in the Bible." That law remained on the books until 1967, when it was swept away on the rising tide of the Black-led movement for democratic and constitutional rights.

It comes as no surprise then that on the hundred-fiftieth anniversary of *The Descent of Man*, the foundations Darwin laid are once again under attack. This time, however, those leading the assault are individuals and institutions parading themselves as "progressives."

Contrary to its name, the magazine *Science*, official publication of the Association for the Advancement of Science, has joined the race-baiting assault on historical figures in many fields. An editorial by Princeton anthropologist Agustín Fuentes in the May 21, 2021, issue charges that, "Darwin thought he was relying on data, objectivity, and scientific thinking in describing human evolutionary outcomes. But for much of the book, he was not. 'Descent,' like so many of the scientific tomes of Darwin's day, offers a racist and sexist view of humanity."

In addition, Fuentes charges, *The Descent of Man* offers "justification of empire and colonialism, and genocide, through 'survival of the fittest.'" Fuentes finds this

Darwin and evolution have been targeted by reactionary and obscurantist forces since mid-1800s. Today the assault is led by individuals and institutions parading as "progressives."

Right: When Darwin published *Descent of Man* in 1871, some dozen years after his pioneering *Origin of Species*, he was ridiculed by London magazine *Hornet*. "A Venerable Orangutang, a Contribution to Unnatural History," read cartoon's caption.

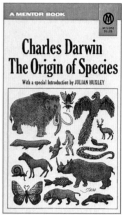

Above: 1925 "Monkey Trial" was headline news across US after court convicted high school teacher John T. Scopes under Tennessee law banning teaching of evolution.

Below: "Progressive" assault today is shown by editorial in May 2021 issue of weekly magazine of the American Association for the Advancement of Science: **"Darwin offers a racist and sexist view of humanity"** and **"justification of empire and colonialism, and genocide."**

"confounding given Darwin's robust stance against slavery," and Darwin's insistence that all "the races of man diverged at an extremely remote epoch from their common progenitor." Yet Darwin was an "*English man*" (emphasis added), Fuentes says, "with injurious and unfounded prejudices that warped his view of data and experience," and students today should be taught that.

A group of evolutionary biologists answered Fuentes in a statement that *Science* editors posted only online:

> What Darwin wrote was of course shaped by Victorian realities and perspectives on sex and racial differences, some still extant today, but this is not a new revelation. Rather than calmly noting these influences, Fuentes repeatedly puts Darwin in the dock for the Victorian sexist and racist norms within which he presented his explosive thesis that humanity evolved. Fuentes incorrectly suggests that Darwin justified genocide. Darwin was frequently and notably more modern in his thinking than most Victorians. In "The Descent" he demolished the slavery-justifying view of different races as separate species, so inspiring the anti-racist perspectives of later anthropologists. . . .
>
> Students taught about the historical context for Darwin's writing should appreciate how revolutionary Darwin's ideas were, challenging many (but not all) prevailing Victorian perspectives. We lament the failure to celebrate the vast impact of those ideas at the expense of the distorting treatment Fuentes offers.

Such historical perspective is useful for readers of *Labor, Nature, and the Evolution of Humanity* to bear in mind. Marx, Engels, and Novack, like their contemporaries, use the terms "savagery," "barbarism," and "civilization" when writing about three main stages of human social evolution. Those were the terms used by anthropologists in the nineteenth and most of the twentieth centuries to denote the earliest human societies based on hunting and gathering (savagery), pre-class agricultural societies (barbarism), and class-divided societies (civilization). The first class societies—whether in Mesopotamia or Egypt, Greece or Rome, or most of Asia—came initially with slavery as the increasingly dominant mode of production, along with the advent of writing, major urban concentrations, and large-scale commerce.

The victorious national liberation struggles of colonial peoples over the past seventy-five years, including fights by oppressed nationalities in the United States and elsewhere in the imperialist countries, have had a profound impact on the consciousness and action of working people worldwide. Terminology used by the founders of anthropology—a product of their times, not ours—has been superseded by other scientific terms. But it is intellectually narrow-minded, ahistorical, and reactionary to refuse to read, study, and build on the contributions to science and culture by previous generations because those bearers of human progress reflected in some of their language the social relations of the societies in which they lived.

"It is very easy to inveigh against slavery and similar things in general terms, and to give vent to high moral indignation at such infamies," wrote Engels in 1877 in a book-length polemic against Eugen Dühring, a self-important German professor with influence in socialist currents of the times. In what has become a classic of the workers movement, titled *Anti-Dühring*, Engels continued: "Unfortunately all that this conveys is only what everyone knows, namely, that these institutions of antiquity are no longer in accord with our present conditions and our sentiments, which these conditions determine. But it does not tell us one word as to how these institutions arose, why they existed, and what role they played in history."

In turning up his nose at Greek civilization "because it was founded on slavery," Engels said, Dühring "might with equal justice reproach the Greeks with having had no steam-engines or electric telegraphs. And when he asserts that our modern wage bondage can only be explained as a somewhat transformed and mitigated heritage of slavery, and not by its own nature (that is, by the economic laws of modern society) . . . with equal justice we might say that wage-labour could only be explained as a mitigated form of cannibalism, which, it is now established, was the universal primitive form of utilisation of defeated enemies."

～

In "The main course of American History," George Novack poses two questions: "What is the main line of American growth since 1492?" and "What has been the most outstanding peculiarity of American history since the coming of the Europeans?"

Despite detours over five centuries of history, he answers, "the main line of American history has consisted in the construction and consolidation of capitalist civilization. . . . Everything in our national history has to be referred to, and linked up with, the process of establishing the capitalist way of life in its most pronounced and, today, its most pernicious form."

As for the main peculiarity, Novack says, it is that "the growth and construction of American society falls entirely within the epoch of the expansion of capitalism on a global scale"—something not true throughout Europe, Asia, or Latin America. All those societies passed through prolonged periods of feudal relations that have left their stamp to this day.

"Look at US general Douglas MacArthur's preservation of that feudal relic, the emperor of Japan, in the aftermath of World War II," Novack notes, "or that Sunday newspaper supplement delight, the monarchy of England."

~

The third main section in this collection, "The Epoch of the Bourgeoisie and the Forging of its Gravediggers," is taken from the Communist Manifesto, published in 1848 as the first great wave of working-class battles broke across Europe. Opening with the words, *"The history of all hitherto existing society is the history of class struggles,"* it offers an explanation of the roots of exploitation and oppression in today's capitalist world, and, above all, a road to emancipation led by and for the exploited and oppressed.

In that regard, the Manifesto, the founding program of the modern communist workers movement, is the polar opposite of views being advanced today by privileged layers of the meritocracy under the banner of "Critical Race Theory," a banner broadly rejected by working people of all hues. One of the most widely publicized expressions of "Critical Race Theory" is the *New York Times*–sponsored 1619 Project in which Nikole Hannah-Jones, its principal organizer, argues that "anti-black racism runs in the very DNA of this country."

US history began, Hannah-Jones says, when the first ship bearing slaves from Africa accidentally landed on the shores of the British colony of Virginia in 1619. The "belief that black people were not merely enslaved but were a slave race [that is, a different species], became the root of the endemic racism that we still cannot purge from this nation to this day," she writes. The extremity of the violence against Black Americans during the Jim Crow era "was a symptom of the psychological mechanism necessary to absolve White Americans of their country's original sin."

Hannah-Jones joins the chorus of those who argue that the driving force behind the entire history of the "Western World," including of the US to this day, has been the ongoing dominance of people with white skin who act on the belief they are a superior "race" entitled to privilege and power ("white supremacy," in the words of many self-proclaimed "social justice warriors").

At the same time, Hannah-Jones's 2019 essay is a virtual patriotic hymn to US bourgeois democracy. Black Americans, she says, have been "foundational to the idea of American freedom" and "to building the richest and most powerful nation in the world." She adds: "It is we who have been the perfecters of this democracy."

The 1619 Project is aptly named. It did not start as history. It began as an offensive to advance a *political* course. It now pretends to be rooted in history. And it happens, additionally, to advance the career aspirations of its promoters. This rewriting of history is *false*, however, both in method and in content. It is also a frontal assault on historical materialism. On Marxism.

It is not racist attitudes, "psychological mechanisms," or ideas—*in fact, it's not ideas of any kind*—that drive human social relations. It is our material conditions of life that shape our ideas.

Karl Marx underlined this truth in his 1873 afterword to the second edition of *Capital*, explaining how he came to the materialist conclusions developed in that book and throughout his lifetime of work. Marx "openly avowed" himself a "pupil of that mighty thinker" Georg W.F. Hegel, whose writings on history, law, religion, logic, the state, and much more were widely influential in nineteenth-century Germany. At the same time, Marx emphasized, "My dia-

Materialist dialectics, evolution, and revolution

Dialectics is nothing more than the science of the general laws of motion and development of nature, human society, and thought.

FREDERICK ENGELS
Dialectics of Nature, 1877

~

Vulgar thought operates with such concepts as capitalism, morals, freedom, workers state, etc., as fixed abstractions, presuming that capitalism is equal to capitalism, morals are equal to morals, etc. Dialectical thinking analyzes all things and phenomena in their continuous change. . . . Dialectical thinking is related to vulgar thinking in the same way that a motion picture is related to a still photograph. . . .

We call our dialectic materialist, since its roots are neither in heaven nor in the depths of our "free will," but in objective reality, in nature. Consciousness grew out of the unconscious, psychology out of physiology, the organic world out of the inorganic, the solar system out of nebulae. . . .

Darwinism, which explained the evolution of species through quantitative transformations passing into qualitative, was the highest triumph of the dialectic in the whole field of organic matter. . . .

Marx, who in distinction from Darwin was a conscious dialectician, discovered a basis for the scientific classification of human societies in the development of their productive forces and the structure of the relations of ownership that constitute the anatomy of society. . . .

Dialectic training of the mind, as necessary to a revolutionary fighter as are finger exercises to a pianist, demands approaching all problems as *processes* and not as *motionless categories.*

LEON TROTSKY
In Defense of Marxism, 1939

lectical method is, in its foundations, not only different from the Hegelian, but exactly opposite to it."

For Hegel, "the process of thinking"—*"the Idea,"* as Hegel called it—"is the creator of the real world, and the real world is only the external appearance of the idea…. The mystification which the dialectic suffers in Hegel's hands," Marx said, was "still the fashion" in the mid-1800s—*both* among voices of the Prussian monarchy and their base of semifeudal landowners, *and* among the throne's more radical bourgeois challengers and self-proclaimed "free thinkers," often dubbed "Young Hegelians."

For backers of Germany's reactionary status quo (to whom Hegel himself "seemed on the whole more inclined," Engels later wrote), "the mystified form" of the dialectic, stressing an illusory sovereign sway of ideas, "seemed to transfigure and glorify what exists"—the Prussian state, that is, and the pre-industrial social relations it defended.

With Hegel, Marx wrote in the 1873 afterword to *Capital*, the movement of history is "standing on its head. It must be inverted, in order to discover the rational kernel within the mystical shell." Once the husk is stripped away, then a truthful "understanding of what exists" reveals a "recognition of its negation, its inevitable destruction; because it regards every historically developed form as being in a fluid state, in motion. . . . It does not let itself be impressed by anything, being in its very essence critical and revolutionary."

"The ideal," Marx wrote, "is nothing but the material world reflected in the mind of man, and translated into forms of thought."

In the late 1830s and early 1840s, for a short but critical period of time, the young Marx and Engels had counted themselves part of this "left Hegelian" current. They soon broke from it politically, however, along the road to being recruited to the working-class movement by communist workers they had come to know and respect in Germany, France, England, and Belgium.

Engels later recalled that during their period of youthful "storm and stress," Marx and he had collaborated on a book to explain their break from Hegelianism but had abandoned the manuscript "all the more willingly as we had achieved our main purpose—self-clarification!" Commenting on that unfinished book, published under the title *The German Ideology* decades after he and Marx had died, Engels wrote that it "consists of an exposition of the materialist conception of history which proves only how incomplete our knowledge of economic history still was at that time."

During those years, writings by the philosopher Ludwig Feuerbach briefly influenced Marx and Engels, as "an intermediate link between Hegelian philosophy" and proletarian communism. Himself a former Young Hegelian, Feuerbach approached the break from the standpoint of a materialist rejection of religion. "We were all Feuerbachians for a moment," Engels wrote in his 1886 work *Ludwig Feuerbach and the End of Classical Germany Philosophy*. But it was a dead end.

For Marx and Engels, Feuerbach's views soon collided with the revolutionary working-class political activity they were increasingly engaged in. The philosopher's outlook, Engels wrote, was helping to spawn petty-bourgeois socialist currents that put "literary phrases in place of scientific knowledge" and "the liberation of mankind by means of 'love' in place of the emancipation of the proletariat through the economic transformation of production."

Coming out of "the dissolution of the Hegelian school," Engels wrote, the only current that "has borne real fruit [is] connected with the name of Marx." That movement, Engels said, "puts an end to philosophy in the realm of history." It recognizes instead that "in modern history at least . . . all political struggles are class struggles, and all struggles by classes for emancipation, despite their necessarily political form—for every class struggle is a political struggle—turn ultimately on the question of *economic* emancipation."

As workers' experience over a century and a half has taught, however, such emancipation can only be won using a *political* instrument, the dictatorship of the proletariat. In their preface to an 1872 edition of the Communist Manifesto, Marx and Engels pointed to the lessons of the Paris Commune a year earlier, where "the proletariat for the first time held political power for two whole months," they wrote.

That heroic struggle and its defeat at the blood-soaked hands of France's capitalist rulers showed that the Manifesto "has in some details become antiquated," Marx and Engels wrote. "One thing especially was proved by the Commune, namely, that 'the working class cannot simply lay hold of the ready-made State machinery, and wield it for its own purposes.'" A *new state* must be brought to power, guided by a revolutionary leadership of the working class and its exploited allies in their millions.

That lesson was confirmed in practice by the greatest pupil of Marx and Engels, V.I. Lenin, who in October 1917 led the Bolshevik party in bringing to power the workers, allied with the peasantry, of Russia's overturned tsarist empire.

And again in the 1950s and 1960s, as Fidel Castro and the Rebel Army leadership mobilized the Cuban masses in establishing a workers state just ninety miles off the shores of the world's mightiest and most brutal imperialist power. It was the state, the revolutionary government, not of any particular movement or organization, as Fidel put it in a March 1964 speech, but of millions wearing "the work shirts of workers and farmers and other men and women of the people."

∾

The fault of the 1619 Project is not simply its anti-materialist foundations, nor even that what it portrays as historical fact is frequently false. Working people and our children must learn the accurate history of the class struggle in the US and internationally, and books by revolutionary leaders published and distributed by Pathfinder Press have been providing that education for decades. But there is no separate "Black history." Or "women's history." Or "labor history," for that matter.

Slavery and all its racist justifications did not drive the development of the United States. Nor did "white supremacy." *It was capitalism.*

Clarifying the unique character of chattel slavery in the US and the Caribbean, in the early 1860s Marx explained that on plantations, "where commercial speculations figure from the start and production is intended for the world market, capitalist production exists, although only in a formal sense, since the slavery of Negroes precludes free wage labor, which is the basis of capitalist production.

"But the business in which slaves are used is conducted by *capitalists*. The mode of production which they introduce has not arisen out of slavery but is grafted onto it."

The institution of chattel slavery in the US and much of the Americas was an anomaly in the capitalist world. It eventually became such a brake on the development of capitalism in the United States that it had to be eliminated, even at the cost of one of the bloodiest wars in world history. "The present struggle between the South and the North is . . . nothing but a struggle between two social systems, the system of slavery and the system of free [wage] labour," Marx wrote in October 1861. The war had "broken out because the two systems can no longer live peacefully side by side on the North American continent. It can only be ended by the victory of one system over the other."

The peoples of Europe, Marx had written a few days earlier, know that "in this contest the highest form of popular self-government till now realized is giving battle to the meanest and most shameless form of man's enslaving in the annals of history." And at the opening of 1862, he welcomed "the natural sympathy the popular classes all over the world ought to feel for the only popular Government in the world."

More than a year into this "inevitable conflict," in August 1862, Marx wrote Engels that he was convinced that when the US government and its Union Army finally "wage the war in earnest" and "have recourse to revolutionary methods," the Confederacy would be decisively defeated. That, in fact, is what the administration of Abraham Lincoln did over the next three years, hesitantly at first but more and more resolutely in face of both military and political necessity.

The Second American Revolution didn't end with the Union victory in the Civil War. During Radical Reconstruction, class battles, often led by freed slaves, were waged by working people, Black and white.

Above: Gen. Ulysses S. Grant (in front of tree) and staff at Union Army headquarters, Virginia, summer 1864. In March Lincoln had appointed Grant general-in-chief, ordering him to crush Robert E. Lee's Army of Northern Virginia, in the very cradle of the Confederacy. By April 1865 the slaveholders' rebellion was defeated.

Below: Election meeting in South, 1868. Popular governments under Radical Reconstruction barred race discrimination; established public schools, universal male suffrage; expanded women's rights and medical access.

The Civil War had become a revolutionary war.

The US government emancipated slaves across the Confederacy in 1863, and during the following year's presidential election, Lincoln rejected mounting cries from bourgeois voices in border states and elsewhere in the North for a disloyal tradeoff—that is, to annul emancipation in return for the slave owners' consent to an immediate peace.

Instead, Lincoln appointed Ulysses S. Grant to serve as general-in-chief of the Union Army, and mandated Grant to lead the Army of the Potomac in *crushing* General Robert E. Lee's Army of Northern Virginia in what had become the cradle of the slaveholders' rebellion, with its capital in Richmond. Between late summer 1864 and spring 1865, the Union Army encircled Lee's troops in Virginia and dealt the Confederate army blow after blow on the battlefield.

On April 9, 1865, in a private home in the village of Appomattox, Lee accepted Grant's quickly penned terms of surrender. With Lee's defeat, military resistance throughout the Confederacy collapsed.

The Second American Revolution extended well beyond the Union victory in the war itself, however. For a dozen years after the fall of the slaveholding Confederacy, hard-fought class battles were waged during Radical Reconstruction. "Black toilers provided leadership in substantial parts of the South both to freed slaves and to exploited farmers and workers who were white," Jack Barnes explains in an excerpt included in these pages.

"By 1877, Radical Reconstruction had gone down to bloody defeat and not only Afro-Americans but the entire working class had suffered what remains the worst setback in its history," writes Farrell Dobbs in another excerpt. The US working class became more deeply divided by the national oppression of Blacks that was institutionalized in the South on new foundations in the bloody aftermath of 1877. Structural racism *does* exist throughout US society. But its continued existence cannot be accounted for by the demise of an outmoded economic institution, chattel slavery, more than a hundred fifty years ago, or by the crushing of Radical Reconstruction. Nor can it be explained by some mythical original sin, or at least post–1619 sin, of "whiteness."

How can such ideas be squared with the fact that in the twenty-first century there is less racism among working people, and greater working-class solidarity across all skin colors and both sexes, than ever before in US history? That progress is a product, above all, of the powerful Black-led battles that destroyed Jim Crow segregation, as well as the massive social movement a few decades earlier that built the industrial unions.

It is the capitalist class and its apologists who have an interest in diverting us from the real source of the divisions we must overcome if working people are to join together in struggle to put an end to the class society in which we live.

～

"Just as Darwin discovered the law of development of organic nature, so Marx discovered the law of development of human history," said Engels in March 1883, speaking at the graveside of his lifelong friend and comrade.

Marx explained that "the degree of economic development attained by a given people or during a given epoch forms the foundation upon which the state institutions, the legal conceptions, art, and even the ideas on religion, of the people concerned have been evolved, and in the light of which they must, therefore, be explained, instead of vice versa, as had hitherto been the case."

After pointing to Marx's irreplaceable contribution to understanding the laws of human history, however, Engels concluded: "Such was the man of science. But this was not even half the man."

"For Marx was before all else a revolutionist," Engels said. "His real mission in life was to contribute, in one way or another, to the overthrow of capitalist society and of the state institutions which it had brought into being, to contribute to the liberation of the modern proletariat, which he was the first to make conscious of its own position and its needs, conscious of the conditions of its emancipation.

"Fighting was his element. And he fought with a passion, a tenacity, and a success such as few could rival."

It is the revolutionary conquest of state power by the working class—*"conscious of its own position and its needs, conscious of the conditions of its emancipation"*—that will open the door to the final battles to build a world based not on exploitation, the degradation of nature, subjugation of women, racism, and war. A world built instead on human solidarity. A socialist world.

That is what a long view of history teaches us.

November 24, 2021

The part played by labor in the transition from ape to man

Frederick Engels

Labor is the source of all wealth, the political economists assert. And it really is the source—next to nature, which supplies it with the material that it converts into wealth. But it is even infinitely more than this. It is the prime basic condition for all human existence, and this to such an extent that, in a sense, we have to say that labor created man himself.

Many hundreds of thousands of years ago, during an epoch, not yet definitely determined, of that period of the earth's history known to geologists as the Tertiary Period, most likely toward the end of it, a particularly highly developed race of anthropoid apes lived somewhere in the tropical zone—probably on a great continent that has now sunk to the bottom of the Indian

This 1876 article, never completed, was first published in German in 1896, a year after Engels's death, and in English in 1934. Engels also included it in his manuscript for Dialectics of Nature, *first published in 1925.*

Ocean. Charles Darwin has given us an approximate description of these ancestors of ours. They were completely covered with hair, they had beards and pointed ears, and they lived in bands in the trees.

When apes began to lose the habit of using their hands to move around and adopted a more erect posture, that was the decisive step in the transition from ape to man.

First, owing to their way of living, which meant that the hands had different functions than the feet when climbing, these apes began to lose the habit of using their hands to walk and adopted a more and more erect posture. This was *the decisive step in the transition from ape to man.*

All extant anthropoid apes can stand erect and move about on their feet alone, but only in case of urgent need and in a very clumsy way. Their natural gait is in a half-erect posture and includes the use of the hands. The majority rest the knuckles of the fist on the ground and, with legs drawn up, swing the body through their long arms, much as someone who is crippled moves on crutches. In general, all the transition stages from walking on all fours to walking on two legs are still to be observed among the apes today. The latter gait, however, has never become more than a makeshift for any of them.

It stands to reason that if erect gait among our hairy ancestors became first the rule and then, in time, a necessity, other diverse functions must, in the meantime, have devolved upon the hands. Already among the apes there is some difference in the way the hands and the feet are employed. In climbing, as mentioned above, the hands and feet have different uses. The hands are used mainly for gathering and holding food in the same way as the fore paws of the lower mammals are used.

Some apes use their hands to build themselves nests in the trees or even to construct roofs between the branches to protect themselves against the weather, as the chimpanzee, for example, does. With their hands they grasp sticks to defend themselves against enemies, or pelt their enemies with fruits and stones. In captivity they use their hands for a number of simple operations copied from human beings.

But it is in this that one sees the great gulf between the undeveloped hand of even the most man-like apes and the human hand that has been highly perfected by hundreds of thousands of years of labor. The number and general arrangement of the bones and muscles are the same in both ape and man, but the hand of the lowest savage can perform hundreds of operations that no simian hand can imitate—no simian hand has ever fashioned even the crudest stone knife.

The hand is not only the organ of labor. It is also the product of labor.

The first operations for which our ancestors gradually learned to adapt their hands during the many thousands of years of transition from ape to man could have been only very simple ones. The lowest savages, even those in whom regression to a more animal-like condition with a simultaneous physical degeneration can be assumed, are nevertheless far superior to these transitional beings. Before the first flint could be fashioned into a knife by human hands, a period of time probably elapsed in comparison with which the historical period known to us appears insignificant.

But the decisive step had been taken—*the hand had become free* and could henceforth attain ever greater dexterity. The greater flexibility thus acquired was inherited and increased from generation to generation.

Thus the hand is not only the organ of labor, *it is also the product of labor.* It is only by labor—by adaptation to ever new operations, through the inheritance of muscles, ligaments, and, over longer periods of time, bones that had undergone special development and the ever-renewed employment of this inherited refinement in new, more and more complicated operations—that the human hand has acquired the high degree of perfection required to conjure into being the paintings of a Raphael, the statues of a Thorwaldsen, the music of a Paganini.

But the hand did not exist alone, it was only one member of an integral, highly complex organism. And what benefited the hand, benefited also the whole body it served; and this in two ways.

In the first place, the body benefited from the law of correlation of growth, as Darwin called it. This law states that certain forms of different parts of an organic being are always bound up with certain forms of other parts of the body that, to all appearances, have no connection with them.

Thus all animals that have red blood cells without cell nuclei, and in which the head is attached to the first vertebra by means of a double articulation (condyles), also without exception possess lacteal glands for suckling their

Labor, along with the nature it transforms, is the source of all wealth. It's the condition for all human existence. In that sense, we can say that labor created man himself.

Depiction of early humans using tools to create a fire.

Through cooperative labor over more than two million years, humans developed food-gathering skills, tools, speech, hunting, and the controlled use of fire. Each of these social conquests was a milestone in the ability of human beings to secure the means of sustenance.

young. Similarly, cloven hoofs in mammals are regularly associated with the possession of a multiple stomach for rumination. Changes in certain forms involve changes in the form of other parts of the body, although we cannot explain the connection. Perfectly white cats with blue eyes are always, or almost always, deaf.

The gradually increasing perfection of the human hand, and the commensurate adaptation of the feet for erect gait, have undoubtedly, by virtue of such correlation, reacted on other parts of the organism. However, this action has not as yet been sufficiently investigated for us to be able to do more here than to state the fact in general terms.

Much more important is the direct, demonstrable influence of the development of the hand on the rest of the organism. It has already been noted that our simian ancestors were gregarious; it is obviously impossible to seek the derivation of man, the most social of all animals, from non-gregarious immediate ancestors.

Mastery over nature, which began with the development of the hand, with labor, widened man's horizon at every new advance. He was continually discovering new, hitherto unknown properties in natural objects. On the other hand, the development of labor necessarily helped to bring the members of society closer together by increasing cases of mutual support and joint activity, and by making clear the advantage of this joint activity to each individual.

In short, men in the making arrived at the point where *they had something to say* to each other. Necessity created the organ. The undeveloped larynx of the ape was slowly but surely transformed by modulation to produce constantly more developed modulation. And the organs of the mouth gradually learned to pronounce one articulate sound after another.

Comparison with animals proves that this explanation of the origin of language from and in the process of labor is the only correct one. The little that even the most highly-developed animals need to communicate to each other does not require articulate speech. In its natural state, no animal feels handicapped by its inability to speak or to understand human speech.

It is quite different when it has been tamed by man. The dog and the horse, by association with man, have developed such a good ear for articulate speech that they easily learn to understand any language within the range of their perception. Moreover, they have acquired the capacity for feelings such as affection for man, gratitude, etc., which were previously foreign to them. Anyone who has had much to do with such animals will hardly be able to escape the conviction that in many cases they *now* feel their inability to speak as a defect, although, unfortunately, it is one that can no longer be remedied because their vocal organs are too specialized in a definite direction.

However, where vocal organs exist, within certain limits even this inability disappears. The buccal organs of birds are as different from those of man as they can be, yet birds are the only animals that can learn to speak.

And it is the bird with the most hideous voice, the parrot, that speaks best of all. Let no one object that the parrot does not understand what it says. It is true that for the sheer pleasure of talking and associating with human beings, the parrot will chatter for hours at a stretch, continually repeating its whole vocabulary. But within the limits of its perception, it can also learn to understand what it is saying. Teach a parrot swear words in such a way that it gets an idea of their meaning (one of the great amusements of sailors returning from the tropics). Tease it and you will soon discover that it knows how to use its swear words just as correctly as a Berlin vegetable peddler. The same is true of begging for tidbits.

> **First labor, then, with it, speech.
> These were the two essential stimuli
> in the process of the ape's brain
> gradually changing into that of man.**

First labor, after it and then with it speech—these were the two most essential stimuli under the influence of which the brain of the ape gradually changed into that of man, which for all its similarity is far larger and more developed.

The brain developed hand in hand with its most immediate instruments—the sense organs. Just as the gradual development of speech is inevitably accompanied by a corresponding refinement of the organ of hearing, so the development of the brain as a whole is accompanied by a refinement of all the senses.

The eagle sees much farther than man, but the human eye discerns considerably more in things than does the eye of the eagle. The dog has a far keener sense of smell than man, but it does not distinguish a hundredth part of the odors that for man are definite signs denoting different things. And the sense of touch, which the ape hardly possesses in its crudest primitive form, has been developed only side by side with the development of the human hand itself, through the medium of labor.

The development of the brain and its attendant senses, the increasing clarity of consciousness and powers of abstraction and reasoning, gave both labor and speech an ever-renewed impulse to further development.

This development did not reach its conclusion when man finally became distinct from the ape, but on the whole made further powerful progress, its degree and direction varying among different peoples and at different times, and here and there even being interrupted by local or temporary regression. This further development has been strongly urged forward, on the one hand, and guided along more definite directions, on the other, by a new element which came into play with the appearance of fully-fledged man, namely, *society.*

Hundreds of thousands of years—of no greater significance in the history of the earth than one second in the life of man—certainly elapsed before human society arose out of a troupe of tree-climbing monkeys.* Yet it did finally appear. And what do we find once more as the characteristic difference between the troupe of apes and human society? *Labor.*

The group of apes was satisfied to browse over the feeding area determined for it by geographical conditions or the resistance of neighboring troupes; it undertook migrations and struggles to win new feeding grounds, but it was incapable of extracting from them more than they offered in their natural state, except that it unconsciously fertilized the soil with its own ex-

---

* A leading authority in this respect, Sir William Thomson, has calculated that *little more than a hundred million years* could have elapsed since the time when the earth had cooled sufficiently for plants and animals to be able to live on it.—FREDERICK ENGELS

[Scientists today estimate the formation of the earth occurred some 4.5 billion years ago, and the first forms of life emerged 700 million to a little more than a billion years later. Engels's conclusion, however, remains true.]

crement. As soon as all possible feeding grounds were occupied, there could be no further increase in the ape population; the number of animals could at best remain stationary.

But all animals waste a great deal of food, and, in addition, destroy in the germ the next generation of the food supply. Unlike the hunter, the wolf does not spare the doe that would provide it with the young the next year. The goats in Greece, which eat away the young bushes before they grow to maturity, have eaten bare all the mountains of the country.

This "despoiling" of nature by animals plays an important part in the gradual transformation of species by forcing them to adapt themselves to other than the usual food, thanks to which their blood acquires a different chemical composition and the whole physical constitution gradually alters, while species that have remained unadapted die out.

There is no doubt that this despoiling contributed powerfully to the transition of our ancestors from ape to man. It must have led to a continual increase in the number of plants used for food and the consumption of more and more edible parts of food plants by a race of apes that far surpassed all others in intelligence and adaptability. In short, food became more and more varied, as did also the substances entering the body with it, substances that were the chemical premises for the transition to man.

But all that was not yet labor in the proper sense of the word. Labor begins with the making of tools. And what are the most ancient tools, judging by the relics of prehistoric man that have been discovered, and by the mode of life of the earliest historical peoples and of the most primitive of contemporary savages? They are hunting and fishing implements, the former at the same time serving as weapons. But hunting and fishing presuppose the transition from an exclusively vegetable diet to the concomitant use of meat, and this is another important step in the process of transition from ape to man.

A *meat diet* contained in an almost ready state the most essential ingredients required by the organism for its metabolism. It shortened the time required for digestion and other vegetative bodily processes analogous to those of plant life, and thus gained further time, material, and desire for the active manifestation of animal life proper. And the farther man in the making moved from the vegetable kingdom the higher he rose above the animal.

Just as becoming accustomed to a vegetable diet side by side with meat converted wild cats and dogs into the servants of man, so also adaptation to a meat diet, side by side with a vegetable diet, greatly contributed toward giving bodily strength and independence to man in the making. The meat diet, however, had its greatest effect on the brain, which now received a far richer flow of the materials necessary for its nourishment, and which therefore could develop more rapidly and perfectly from generation to generation.

With all due respect to the vegetarians man did not come into existence without a meat diet, and if the latter, among all peoples known to us, has led to cannibalism at some time or other (the forefathers of the Berliners, the Weletabians or Wilzians, used to eat their parents as late as the tenth century), that is of no consequence to us today.

The meat diet led to two new advances of decisive importance—the harnessing of fire and the domestication of animals. The first further shortened the digestive process, as it provided the mouth with food already, as it were, half-

TIMELINE OF HUMAN EVOLUTION

ANIMAL RAISING,
AGRICULTURE

10–15,000 years ago

MORE ADVANCED
POTTERY AND ART

50,000 years ago

SHELTER,
CLOTHING

400,000 years ago

HUNTING, USE OF FIRE

1.9 million years ago

POSSIBLE EARLIEST SPEECH

2.2 million years ago

TOOL USE

2.4 million years ago

WALKING UPRIGHT

6 million years ago

FIRST HUMANS

*FIRST BIPEDAL
HUMAN ANCESTORS*

HOMO HABILIS
(2.4 MILLION)

NEANDERTHALS
(400,000)

HOMO
ERECTUS
(1.9 MILLION)

HOMO
SAPIENS
(300,000)

(6 MILLION)

6	5	4	3	2	1	0

Millions of years

digested. The domestication of animals made meat more copious by opening up a new, more regular source of supply in addition to hunting. It moreover provided, in milk and its products, a new article of food at least as valuable as meat in its composition.

Thus, both these advances were, in themselves, new means for the emancipation of man. It would lead us too far afield to dwell here in detail on their indirect effects notwithstanding the great importance they have had for the development of man and society.

Just as man learned to consume everything edible, he also learned to live in any climate. He spread over the whole of the habitable world, being the only animal fully able to do so of its own accord. The other animals that have become accustomed to all climates—domestic animals and vermin—did not become so independently, but only in the wake of man.

And the transition from the uniformly hot climate of the original home of man to colder regions, where the year was divided into summer and winter, created new requirements—shelter and clothing as protection against cold and damp—and hence new spheres of labor, new forms of activity, which further and further separated man from animals.

By the combined functioning of hand, speech organs and brain, not only in each individual but also in society, men became capable of executing more and more complicated operations, and were able to set themselves, and achieve, higher and higher aims. The work of each generation itself became different, more perfect and more diversified.

Agriculture was added to hunting and cattle raising; then came spinning, weaving, metalworking, pottery and navigation. Along with trade and industry, art and science finally appeared. Tribes developed into nations and states. Law and politics arose, and with them that imaginary reflection of human things in the human mind—religion.

In face of all these creations, which at first appeared to be products of the mind and seemed to dominate human societies, the more modest productions of the working hand retreated into the background. That was especially true because the mind that planned the labor was able, at a very early stage in the development of society (for example, already in the primitive family), to have that labor carried out by other hands than its own. All merit for the swift advance of civilization was ascribed to the mind, to the development and activity of the brain.

Men became accustomed to explain their actions as arising out of thought instead of their needs (which in any case are reflected and perceived in the mind). And so, in the course of time there emerged that idealistic world outlook, which, especially since the fall of the world of antiquity, has dominated men's minds. It still rules them to such a degree that even the most materialistic natural scientists of the Darwinian school are still unable to form any clear idea of the origin of man, because under this ideological influence they do not recognize the part that has been played therein by labor.

Animals, as has already been pointed out, change the environment by their activities in the same way, even if not to the same extent, as man does, and these changes, as we have seen, in turn react upon and change those who made them. In nature nothing takes place in isolation. Everything affects and is affected by every other thing, and it is mostly because this manifold motion and interaction is forgotten that our natural scientists are prevented from gaining a clear insight into the simplest things.

We have seen how goats have prevented the regeneration of forests in Greece. On the island of St. Helena [in the Atlantic], goats and pigs brought by the first arrivals have succeeded in wiping out its old vegetation almost completely, and so have prepared the ground for the spreading of plants brought by later sailors and colonists.

Even scientists of the Darwin school present no clear idea of the origin of man because they cannot recognize the role played by labor in it.

But animals exert a lasting effect on their environment unintentionally and, as far as the animals themselves are concerned, accidentally. The further removed men are from animals, however, the more their effect on nature assumes the character of premeditated, planned action directed toward definite preconceived ends.

The animal destroys the vegetation of a locality without realizing what it is doing. Man destroys it in order to sow field crops on the soil thus released, or to plant trees or vines which he knows will yield many times the amount planted. He transfers food plants and domestic animals from one country to another and thus changes the flora and fauna of whole continents.

What's more, through artificial breeding both plants and animals are so changed by the hand of man that they become unrecognizable. The wild plants from which our grain varieties originated are still being sought in vain. There is still some dispute about the wild animals from

'Our social being determines our consciousness'

In the social production of their life, men inevitably enter into definite relations that are independent of their will—relations of production that correspond to a definite stage of development of their material productive forces.

The sum total of these relations of production constitutes the economic structure of society, the real foundation, on which rises a legal and political superstructure and to which correspond definite forms of social consciousness.

The mode of production of material life conditions the social, political, and intellectual life process in general. It is not the consciousness of men that determines their being, but, on the contrary, their social being that determines their consciousness.

At a certain stage of their development, the material productive forces of society come in conflict with the existing relations of production or—what is but a legal expression of the same thing—with the property relations within which they have been at work hitherto.

From forms of development of the productive forces, these relations turn into their fetters. Then begins an epoch of social revolution. . . .

No social formation ever perishes before all the productive forces for which there is room in it have developed. And new, higher relations of production never appear before the material conditions of their existence have matured in the womb of the old society itself.

KARL MARX, 1859
A Contribution to the Critique of Political Economy

which our very different breeds of dogs or our equally numerous breeds of horses are descended.

It goes without saying that it would not occur to us to dispute the ability of animals to act in a planned, premeditated fashion. On the contrary, a planned mode of action exists in embryo wherever protoplasm, living albumen, exists and reacts, that is, carries out definite, even if extremely simple, movements as a result of definite external stimuli. Such reaction takes place even where there is yet no cell at all, far less a nerve cell. There is an appearance of a planned action in the way insect-eating plants capture their prey, although they do it quite unconsciously.

In animals the capacity for conscious, planned action is proportional to the development of the nervous system, and among mammals it attains a fairly high level. While fox-hunting in England one can always observe how unerringly the fox makes use of its excellent knowledge of the locality in order to elude its pursuers, and how well it knows and turns to account all favorable features of the ground that cause the scent to be lost.

Among our domestic animals, more highly developed thanks to association with man, one can constantly observe acts of cunning on exactly the same level as those of children. For, just as the development history of the human embryo in the mother's womb is only an abbreviated repetition of the history, extending over millions of years, of the bodily development of our animal ancestors, starting from the worm, so the mental development of the human child is only a still more abbreviated repetition of the intellectual development of these same ancestors, at least of the later ones.

But all the planned action of all animals has never succeeded in impressing the stamp of their will upon the earth. That was left for man.

> **Let us not, however, flatter ourselves overmuch on account of our human victories over nature. For each such victory nature takes its revenge on us.**

In short, the animal merely *uses* its environment, and brings about changes in it simply by its presence; man by his changes makes it serve his ends, *masters* it. This is the final, essential distinction between man and other animals, and once again it is labor that brings this about.

Let us not, however, flatter ourselves overmuch on account of our human victories over nature. For each such victory nature takes its revenge on us. Each victory, it is true, in the first place brings about the results we expected, but in the second and third places it has quite different, unforeseen effects which only too often cancel the first.

The people who, in Mesopotamia, Greece, Asia Minor and elsewhere, destroyed the forests to obtain cultivable land never dreamed that by removing along with the forests the collecting centers and reservoirs of moisture they were laying the basis for the present desolation of those lands.

When the Italians of the Alps used up the pine forests on the southern slopes, so carefully cherished on the northern slopes, they had no inkling that by doing so they were cutting at the roots of the dairy industry in their region. They had still less inkling that they were thereby depriving their mountain springs of water for the greater part of the year, and making it possible for them to pour still more furious torrents on the plains during the rainy seasons.

Those who spread the potato in Europe were not aware that with these mealy tubers they were at the same time spreading scrofula.*

Thus at every step we are reminded that we by no means rule over nature like a conqueror over a foreign people, like someone standing outside nature. We, on the contrary, with flesh, blood and brain, belong to nature, and exist in its midst. And all our mastery of it consists in the fact that we have the advantage over all other creatures of being able to learn its laws and apply them correctly.

And, in fact, with every day that passes we are acquiring a better understanding of these laws and getting to perceive both the more immediate and the more long-term consequences of our interference with the normal course of nature. In particular, after the mighty advances made by the natural sciences in the present century, we are more than ever in a position to realize, and hence to control, the more long-term natural consequences of at least our most common productive activities.

But the more this progresses, the more will men not only feel but also know their oneness with nature. And the more inconceivable will become the senseless and unnatural idea of a contradiction between mind and matter, man and nature, soul and body, such as arose after the decline

---

* Probably a form of tuberculosis. A widely held belief, later disproved.

The Spanish planters in Cuba burned down forests on mountain slopes and obtained fertilizer from the ashes for very profitable coffee harvests. What cared they that the tropical rainfall afterward washed away the unprotected topsoil?

Right: Deforestation in colonial Brazil, early 1800s.

Capitalists, writes Engels, are driven to "concern themselves only with the most immediate benefits of their actions"—their profits—not the longer-term effects.

Left: Workers tend saplings in a tree nursery in Las Tunas province, eastern Cuba, 2016. Safeguarding the environment is a priority of Cuba's working people and their revolutionary government. Some 95 percent of the island's forests are protected—the highest proportion in the world.

of classical antiquity in Europe and obtained its highest elaboration in Christianity.

It required the labor of thousands of years for us to learn a little of how to calculate the more long-term *natural* effects of our actions in the field of production, but it has been still more difficult in regard to the more remote *social* effects of these actions.

We mentioned the potato and the resulting spread of scrofula. But what is scrofula compared to the effects that reducing workers to a potato diet had on the living conditions of the popular masses in whole countries? Or compared to the famine the potato blight brought to Ireland in 1847, which consigned to the grave a million Irishmen, nourished solely or almost exclusively on potatoes, and forced the emigration overseas of two million more?

When the Arabs learned to distill spirits, it never entered their heads that by so doing they were creating one of the chief weapons for the annihilation of the aborigines of the then still undiscovered American continent. And when afterward Columbus discovered this America, he did not know that by doing so he was giving a new lease of life to slavery, which in Europe had long ago been done away with, and laying the basis for the Negro slave trade.

The men who in the seventeenth and eighteenth centuries labored to create the steam-engine had no idea that they were preparing the instrument which more than any other was to revolutionize social relations throughout the world. Especially in Europe, by concentrating wealth in the hands of a minority and dispossessing the huge majority, this instrument was destined at first to give social and political domination to the bourgeoisie. But later, however, it gave rise to a class struggle between bourgeoisie and proletariat that can end only in the overthrow of the bourgeoisie and the abolition of all class antagonisms.

But in this sphere too, by long and often cruel experience and by collecting and analyzing historical material, we are gradually learning to get a clear view of the indirect, more remote social effects of our production activity, and so are afforded an opportunity to control and regulate these effects as well. This regulation, however, requires something more than mere knowledge.

It requires a complete revolution in our hitherto existing mode of production, and simultaneously a revolution in our whole contemporary social order.

All hitherto existing modes of production have aimed merely at achieving the most immediately and directly useful effect of labor. The further consequences, which appear only later and become effective through gradual repetition and accumulation, were totally neglected.

The original common ownership of land corresponded, on the one hand, to a level of development of human beings in which their horizon was restricted in general to what lay immediately available, and presupposed, on the other hand, a certain abundance of land that would allow some latitude for correcting the possible bad results of this primeval type of economy. When this surplus land was exhausted, common ownership also declined.

All higher forms of production, however, led to the division of the population into different classes and thereby to the antagonism of ruling and oppressed classes. Thus the interests of the ruling class became the driving factor of production, since production was no longer restricted to providing the barest means of subsistence for the oppressed people.

This has been put into effect most completely in the capitalist mode of production prevailing today in Western Europe. The individual capitalists, who dominate production and exchange, are able to concern themselves only with the most immediate benefits of their actions. Indeed, even this useful effect—inasmuch as it is a question of the usefulness of the article that is produced or exchanged— retreats far into the background, and the sole incentive becomes the profit to be made on selling.

~

Classical political economy, the social science of the bourgeoisie, in the main examines only social effects of human actions in the fields of production and exchange that are actually intended. This fully corresponds to the social organization of which it is the theoretical expression.

As individual capitalists are engaged in production and exchange for the sake of the immediate profit, only the nearest, most immediate results must first be taken into account. As long as the individual manufacturer or merchant sells a manufactured or purchased commodity with the usual coveted profit, he is satisfied and does not concern himself with what afterward becomes of the commodity and its purchasers. The same thing applies to the natural effects of the same actions.

What cared the Spanish planters in Cuba, who burned down forests on the slopes of the mountains and obtained from the ashes sufficient fertilizer for *one* generation of very highly profitable coffee trees—what cared they that the heavy tropical rainfall afterward washed away the unprotected topsoil, leaving behind only bare rock!

In relation to nature, as to society, the present mode of production is predominantly concerned only about the immediate, the most tangible result.

And yet surprise is then expressed when the longer-term effects of actions turn out to be quite different from their objectives, and mostly quite the opposite.

Control over the social effects of our productive activity will require a revolution in our mode of production and in our whole social order.

Since the early 1960s, Cuba's socialist revolution has set an example of what workers and farmers can accomplish when they take state power and use it in the interests of the vast majority.

Above: Thousands demonstrate in Havana backing revolutionary government's nationalization of US and other imperialist-owned properties in Cuba, August 1960. Coffins bearing names of major imperialist companies were tossed into the sea.

Below: "Workers in power," reads banner, as working people mobilize in Havana on May Day, 1961.

When the harmony between supply and demand is transformed into the very opposite, as shown by the course of each ten-year industrial cycle—even in Germany, which has had a little preliminary experience of it in the "crash" [the 1873 world financial crisis and years-long economic depression].

When private ownership based on one's own labor must of necessity develop into workers' lack of property, while all wealth becomes more and more concentrated in the hands of non-workers. When [*Here the manuscript ends.*]

How humanity climbed to civilization

George Novack

I propose first to trace the main line of human development, from our remote animal ancestors to the present, when humanity has become lord of the earth but not yet master of its own creations, not to mention its own social system. After that, I will deal with the central course of evolution in that specific segment of society that occupies much of North America and represents the most developed form of capitalist society.

I will try to show not only how our national history is related to world development but also how we, collectively and individually, fit into the picture. This is a broad and bold undertaking, a sort of jet-propelled journey through the stratosphere of world history. It is forced upon us by the urge to grasp the whole vast spread of events and to understand our specific place within them, as well as by

The first of two talks given in September 1955 at the Socialist Workers Party's West Coast school and camp, held near Los Angeles, California.

69

the very dynamic of scientific theory in sociology, which has its highest expression in Marxism. The movement based upon scientific socialism, which prepares most energetically for the future, likewise must probe most deeply into the past.

~

I shall start from the political case history of an individual. In January 1935 a book appeared which set the style for a series of reflective reports on the trends of our times. It had considerable influence upon radicalized intellectuals here until the outbreak of the Second World War. That book, *Personal History,* was written by Vincent Sheean. This autobiography was a serious effort to find out what the historical events that marked his generation were leading to and what his attitude should be toward their mainstream and crosscurrents.

Sheean told how he started as an ignorant student at the University of Chicago at the close of the First World War. He knew as little about the fundamental forces at work in the world then as millions like him today who are encased in a similar provincialism. As he remarked:

> The bourgeois system insulated all its children as much as possible from a knowledge of the processes of human development, and in my case succeeded admirably in its purpose. Few Hottentots or South Sea Islanders could have been less prepared for life in the great world than I was at twenty-one.

This innocent American went abroad as a newspaperman and learned from the great events of the twenties. He observed the effects of the First World War and the Russian Revolution; he witnessed the stirrings in the Near East, in

Morocco and Palestine—precursors of the vast colonial disturbances after the Second World War. He was also a spectator and played an incidental role in the defeated second Chinese revolution of 1926–27. His experiences were topped by the economic collapse of capitalism after 1929 and the spread of fascism in Europe.

These upheavals jolted Sheean from his doze, opened his eyes, and propelled him toward Marxism and the revolutionary socialist movement. He was swept along in the swirling torrent of that first stage in the crack-up of capitalist civilization—and began to recognize it as such. Great social, economic, and political events exposed the bankruptcy of the ideas about the world he had acquired through his middle-class education in the Midwest and impelled him to cast them off.

Sheean found in Marxism the most convincing explanation of the processes of social development and the causes of the decisive events of his own age. He was inspired by its ability to answer the question that besets every thinking person: What relation does my own life have to those who have preceded me on this earth, all my contemporaries, and the incalculable generations who will come later?

Scientific, political, and moral considerations combined to attract him to the science of the socialist movement. Sheean admired Marxism, he emphasized, because it took "the long view." This is not a phrase he coined, but one he borrowed from a participant in the struggle. Marxists, he noted, were or should be guided not by partial views and episodic considerations but by the most comprehensive outlook over the expanse of biological evolution and human achievement.

The all-embracing synthesis of history offered by Marxism contrasted sharply with the worm's-eye view he had

had in the Midwest. The United States had the most up-to-date gadgets, but it was dominated by extremely old-fashioned ideas about social evolution.

Sheean had caught on to one of the outstanding features of that system of thought that bears the name of its creator, Karl Marx. Scientific socialism does provide the most consistent, many-sided, and far-reaching of all the doctrines of evolution—and revolution. So far as it is possible, the "long view" it presents is the march of mankind seen in its full scope, its current reality, and its ultimate consequences.

~

What was this long view that attracted Vincent Sheean and so many millions before him and since? What can a review of the process of evolution, analyzed by Marxism's materialist methods, teach us about the way things change in this world?

We can single out four critical turning points in the timetable of evolution. The first was the origin of our planet about three or four billion years ago. The second was the emergence of life in the form of simple one-celled sea organisms about two and a half billion years ago. (These are only approximate but commonly accepted dates at the present time.) Third was the appearance of the first backboned animals about four to five hundred million years ago. Last was the evolution of what became the human species, within the past several million years.

Let us begin with the third great chapter in this historical panorama—the first fish species. The American Museum of Natural History has prepared a chart that portrays the principal stages in organic evolution from the first fish up to ourselves, the highest form of mammalian creatures. The backbone introduced by the fish was one of the basic structures for subsequent higher evolution.

Astraspis, as one of the first vertebrate specimens is called, lived in the Paleozoic era near present-day Cañon City, Colorado, where its plates were found in delta deposits. This native American of four to five hundred million years ago was very revolutionary for its day. Here is what a popular authority, Brian Curtis, says about this development in *The Life Story of the Fish:*

> An animal with a backbone does not seem strange to us today. But at the time that the first fish appeared upon earth, which we know from geological records to have been roughly five hundred million years ago, he must have seemed a miraculous thing. He was the very latest model in animal design, a radical, one might almost say a reckless experiment of that force which we find it convenient to personify as Mother Nature.

What did its "radicalism" consist of?

> For up to that time no creature had ever been made with the hard parts inside instead of outside. . . . Nature might be said to have had a brainstorm, abandoned all the earlier methods and turned out overnight something absolutely new and unheard of.

Although the fish retained some of the old external armor, what was decisive from the standpoint of evolution was its acquisition of the backbone. This converted the fish into a creature basically different from anything living before. Thus, the new backboned type both *grew out of* the old and *outgrew* it. But that is not all. It then went on to conquer new realms of existence and activity. The most revolutionary feature of the fish was the fact that it became the starting point for the entire hierarchy of back-boned creatures.

These first vertebrates subsequently advanced from the fish through the amphibians (which lived both in water and on land), through the reptiles, and finally branched off into the warm-blooded creatures: birds and mammals. Mankind is today the most advanced point of mammalian development. This much of animal evolution is accepted by all scientific authorities.

But these ideas and facts, so commonplace today, were the subversive thoughts of yesterday. We readily adopt this scientific view of organic evolution without realizing that this very act of acceptance is part of a reversal in human thinking about the world and the creatures in it, which has taken place on a mass scale only during the past century. Recall, for example, the prevalence of the biblical myth of creation in the Western world up to a few generations ago.

Two aspects of the facts about the vertebrates deserve special discussion. First, the transfer of the bony parts of the fish from the outside to the inside embodied a qualitatively new form of organic structure, a break in the continuity of development up to that time, a jump onto a higher level of life. Every biologist acknowledges this fact.

But this fact has a more profound significance, which tells us much about the methods of evolutionary change in general. It demonstrates how, at the critical point in the accumulation of changes outside and inside an organism, the conflicting elements that compose it break up the old form of its existence, and the progressive formation passes over, by way of a leap, to a qualitatively new and historically higher state of development. This is true not only of organic species but of social formations and systems of thought as well.

The most revolutionary feature of the fish was its backbone. That was the starting point for all later creatures.

Over millions of years, vertebrates—animals with a backbone—evolved from fish to amphibians, reptiles, birds, and mammals.

Above: Artist's depiction of *Tiktaalik,* a freshwater fish that lived about 375 million years ago. Its fossilized remains help document the progression from fish to land-dwelling animals.

This radical overturn is undeniable in the case of the birth and evolution of the fish and its ultimate surpassing by higher species. But it is much harder for many people to accept such a conclusion when it comes to the transformation of a lower social organization into a higher social organization. This reluctance to consistently apply the teachings of evolution to all things, and above all to the capitalist social system in which we live, is rooted in the determination of its rulers to defend powerful but obsolete and narrow class interests against opposing class forces and rival ideas that aim to create a genuinely new order of things.

The second point to be stressed is the fact that the fish, as the first vertebrate, occupies a specific place in the sequence of the evolution of organisms. It is one link in a chain of the manifestations of life extending from one-celled protozoa to the most complex organisms. This first creature with a backbone came out of a host of creatures that never had such a skeletal structure. In turn, it gave rise to superior orders that had this and much more.

Contradictory as it is, many scholars and scientists who take the order of evolution of organic species for granted, stubbornly resist the extension of the same lawfulness to the changing species of social organizations. They will not admit that there has been, or can be, any definite and discernible sequence in the social development of mankind analogous to the steps in the progress from the invertebrates to the fish, through the reptile and mammalian creatures, up to the advent of mankind.

In the present century, this skepticism is especially pronounced among sociologists in our own country. Thinkers of this type, of course, know that there have been many changes in history, that many diverse formations are found in the fields of anthropology, archaeology, history, sociology, and politics.

What they deny is that these typical manifestations of social life can—or even should—be arranged in any determinate order of historical development in which each has its given place from the beginning to the end, from the lower to the higher, determined by the productivity of social labor. They teach that all the various forms of culture and ways of life are merely dissimilar to one another and that it is impossible or unnecessary to try to discover any regular sequence or lawful affiliation in their emergence.

This view and method is thoroughly antievolutionary, antiscientific, and essentially reactionary. But it is explainable. The denial of the possibility of finding out the order of advancement in social structures springs—if you will permit the analogy—from the resistance by today's invertebrates to the oncoming vertebrates who represent a superior form of organization and are destined to supplant them in the struggle for social survival.

The evolutionary record itself, starting with the upward climb of the fish, most effectively refutes this tenacious conservatism. The first vertebrate was followed by six further progressive types of fish in the next hundred million years. The most advanced was a freshwater, medium-sized carnivorous species whose fossils have been found in Canada. Although this specimen spent much of its life in the water, it had acquired many of the functions required for living on land. Fish, as you know, are customarily at home in water, breathe through gills, and have fins. It was unbecoming to established fish-nature for the first amphibians to get up out of the water and crawl onto land, breathe through lungs, and move about on legs.

Let us imagine a fish (if you will go along with the fancy) who looked backward rather than forward, as some fish do. This backward-looking fish could exclaim to the forward-moving amphibians: "We fish, the oldest inhabitants, have never before done such things; they can't be done; they shouldn't be done!" And, when the amphibians persisted, could shriek: "These things mustn't be done; it's subversive of the good old order to do them!" However, the resistance of inertia did not prevent some water dwellers from turning into land animals.

Animal life continued to move forward as species were modified and transmuted in response to decisive changes in their genetic constitutions and natural habitats. Amphibians turned into reptiles, which had better developed brains, were rib-breathing, egg-laying, had limbs for locomotion, and well-developed eyes. The reptile kingdom evolved gradually toward the mammal, with transitional types that had features belonging to both, until once again a full-fledged new order stepped into the world.

About 135 million years ago, the animal prototype that gave rise to our own tree-living ancestor emerged. This was a rodent-like creature who took another big leap in evolutionary adaptation and activity by quitting the land for the trees. Arboreal existence over six hundred thousand years so altered our animal ancestors from head to toe, from grasping functions to teeth changes, that they elevated themselves to monkey and ape forms. The kinship of the latter with our own kind is so close that it is difficult to distinguish an embryo of the highest apes from that of a human.

The natural conditions had at last been created for the emergence of mankind. It seems likely that changes in climate and geographical conditions drove certain species of primates down from the trees, out of the forests, and onto the plains. A series of important anatomical developments paved the way for the making of the human race. The shortening of the pelvic bone made it possible for the primate to stand erect, to differentiate forelimbs from hind limbs, and to emancipate the hands. The brain became enlarged. Binocular vision and vocal organs made human sight and speech possible.

The central biological organ for the making of mankind was the hand. The hands became opposed to the legs, and the thumb became opposed to the four fingers. This opposition between the thumb and the other fingers has been one of the most fruitful and dynamic of all the unions of opposites in the evolution of humanity. The thumb's ability to counterpose itself to each of the other fingers gave the hand exceptional powers of grasping and manipulating objects and endowed it with extreme flexibility and sensitivity. This acquisition made possible the biological combination of hand-eye-brain. Combined with the prolonged period of care by the mother for her offspring, the natural prerequisites for social life were at hand.

∽

At this point something should be said about the most common argument against socialism: "You can't change human nature!" How much substance is there to this contention?

Once the record of organic evolution is accepted, one proposition, at least, inevitably flows from it: *Fish nature can be changed!* It has been changed into amphibian, reptile, bird, mammalian, and, ultimately, into human natures. The salt in our bodies is one reminder, among many, of our descent from great-grandfather fish in the oceans of ages ago.

This poses the following pertinent questions to the social-change resisters: If fish can change, or be changed so much, on what grounds can narrow restrictions be imposed upon the changeability of mankind? Did our species

From development of the hand to ability to transform nature

When, after thousands of years of struggle, the differentiation of hand from foot, and erect gait, were finally established, man became distinct from the ape. The basis was laid for the development of articulate speech and the mighty development of the brain that has since made the gulf between man and monkey an unbridgeable one.

The specialization of the hand—this implies the tool. And the tool implies the transforming reaction of man on nature: production. Man alone has succeeded in impressing his stamp on nature.

Step by step, with the development of the hand went that of the brain. First of all, consciousness of the conditions for separate, practically useful actions. And later, insight into the natural laws governing them.

The more human beings become removed from animals in the narrower sense of the word, the more they make their own history consciously, the less becomes the influence of unforeseen effects and uncontrolled forces.

FREDERICK ENGELS, 1883
The Dialectics of Nature

lose its plasticity, its potentialities for radical alteration somewhere along the line from the transition of the primate to the human?

The contrary is the case. In the passage to humanity, our species not only retained all the capacities for progressive change inherent in animality but multiplied them to an infinitely higher degree, lifting them onto an entirely new dimension through previously unknown ways and means of evolutionary progress.

It required four to five hundred million years to create the biological conditions necessary for the generation of the first subhumans. This was not brought about through anyone's forethought or foresight, or in accord with any plan, or with the aim of realizing some preconceived goal. It happened, we may say, as the lawful outcome of a series of blind and accidental developments in the forms of natural life. These were spurred forward in the struggle for survival, which eventually culminated in the production of a special kind of primate equipped with the capacities for acquiring more than animal powers.

At this juncture, about six million or so years ago, the most radical of all the transmutations of life on this planet took place. The emergence of mankind embodied something totally different, which became the root of a unique line of development. What was this? It was the passage from animal separatism to human collectivism—from purely biological modes of behavior to the use of acquired social powers.

Where did these added artificial powers come from? Powers that have marked off emerging mankind from all other animal species, elevated our species above the other primates, and made mankind into the dominant order of life? Our dominance is indisputable because we command the power to destroy ourselves and all other forms of life, not to speak of changing them.

The fundamentally new powers mankind acquired were the powers of production, of securing the means of sustenance through the use of tools and joint labor, and sharing the results with one another. I can do no more than single out four of the most important factors in this process.

The first was associated activities in getting food and dividing it.

The second was the use, and later the manufacture, of implements for that purpose.

The third was the development of speech and of reasoning, which arose from and was promoted by living and working together.

The fourth was the use, the domestication, and the production of fire. Fire was the first natural force, the first chemical process, put to socially productive use by ascending humanity.

Thanks to these new powers, emerging mankind enormously speeded up the changes in our own species and later in the world around us. The historical record of the past million years is essentially one of the formation and continual transformation of humanity. This in turn has promoted the transformation of the world around us.

What has enabled us to effect such colossal changes in ourselves and our environment? All the biological changes in our stock over the past million years, taken together, have not been a prominent factor in the advancement of the human species. Yet during that time humanity has taken the raw material inherited from our animal past, socialized it, humanized it, and partially, though not completely, civilized it. The axis of human development, contrasted to animality, revolves around these social rather than biological processes.

The mainspring of this progress comes from the improvement of the powers of production, acquired along the way and expanded in accordance with man's growing needs. By discovering and utilizing the diverse properties and resources of the world around us, mankind has gradually added to our ability to produce the

What marked off emerging humanity from all other animal species was the power of production, the power of associated labor, and the use of tools, in securing and sharing food.

Human beings improved their ability to secure food as they advanced over millennia from hunting and gathering to the domestication of animals and cultivation of crops.

Above: Depiction of hunting and dancing, painted between 6000 and 3000 BC in Magura cave, Bulgaria.

Below: Farmers drawing water from Egypt's Nile River for irrigation, about 2000 BC.

means of life. As these have developed, all other social powers—the power of speech, of thought, of art, and of science, etc.—have been enhanced.

> **The decisive difference between the highest animals and ourselves is our development of the means and forces of production and destruction, two aspects of the same phenomenon.**

The decisive difference between the highest animals and ourselves is to be found in our development of the means and forces of production and destruction, two aspects of one and the same phenomenon. This accounts not only for the qualitative difference between human beings and the other animals but also for the specific differences between one level of human development and another. What demarcates the peoples of the Stone Age from those of the Iron Age, and savage life from civilized societies, is the difference in the total powers of production at their disposal.

What happens when there is a test of strength between two different levels of productive and destructive power was dramatically illustrated when the Spanish conquerors invaded the Western Hemisphere. The indigenous peoples were armed with bows and arrows and slings; the newcomers had muskets and gunpowder. The Indians had canoes and paddles; the Spaniards had big sailing ships. The Indians wore leather or padded jackets for protection in warfare; the Spaniards had steel armor. The Indians had no domesticated draught animals but went on foot; the

Spaniards rode horses. Their superior equipment inspired terror and enabled the conquistadors with inferior manpower to defeat their antagonists.

This basic proposition of historical materialism should be easier for us to grasp because we are privileged to witness the first stage of a technological revolution comparable in importance to the taming of fire nearly two million years ago. That is the acquisition of control over the processes of nuclear fission and fusion. This new source of power has already revolutionized the relations among governments and the art of warfare; it is about to transform industry, agriculture, medicine, and many other departments of social activity.

What brought about this technological revolution? Mankind underwent no biological changes in the preceding period. Nor were there any sudden alterations in human modes of thinking, in their sentiments, or their moral ideas. This incalculably powerful force of production and destruction issued from the entire previous development of society's productive forces and all the scientific knowledge and instruments connected with them. Atomic power, with both its productive and destructive capacities, is the latest link in the chain of acquired powers that can be traced back to the earliest elements of social production: associated labor in securing the necessities of life, tool using and making, speech, thought, and fire.

~

Let us come back to that remarkable organ of ours, the hand. The hand, which among the primates originally conveyed food to the mouth, was converted by humanity into an organ for grasping and guiding the materials used and then shaped for tools. The hand is the biological prototype of the tool and the handle; it is the prerequisite and parent of laboring activity. The passage from the hand to the tool coincides with the creation of society and the progressive development of humanity and its latent powers.

The connection between the most rudimentary tools and the complex material instruments of production in today's industrial system has been graphically illustrated in a chart prepared for the DoAll Corporation, of Des Plaines, Illinois, sponsor of a traveling exhibit on "How Basic Tools Created Civilization." This exhibit, which claims to be "the first attempt ever made to assemble the complete history of man's tools," documents the stages in the progress of technology.

The first known tools created by man, called eoliths, date back, some scientists say, to one and a half million years ago. These were sections of broken stone with edges useful for cutting meat, scraping hides, or digging for roots. They were little more than simple extensions of the hand. They were not designed for specific functions but were adaptable for pounding, throwing, scraping, drilling, cutting, etc.

In the next stage, tools underwent improvement along two main lines: their cutting edges were made more efficient; and they became fashioned for special purposes. Men learned to chip stone to a predetermined shape, thereby producing a sharper cutting edge. A wider variety of working tools, such as axes, sharp-pointed drills, thin-edged blades, chisels, and other forerunners of today's hand tools, came into existence.

These tools reduced the time needed to produce sustenance and shelter, thereby raising the social level of production and improving living conditions. Moreover, these new productive activities enhanced man's mental capacities. The complexity of special-purpose tools indicates the development of a mentality capable of understanding the necessity of producing the *means* before the *end* could be attained. Mental concepts of specific use preceded both the design and construction of these special-purpose tools.

Each of the subsequent steps in the improvement of tool use and making likewise resulted in the economizing of labor time, an increased productivity of labor, better living conditions, and the growth of intellectual abilities. The motor force of human history comes from the greater productivity of labor made possible by decisive advances in the techniques and tools of production.

This can be seen in the development of hunting. At first, mankind could as a rule capture only small and slow animals. Regular consumption of big game was made possible by the invention of such hunting weapons as the thrusting spear, the throwing spear, the spear-thrower, and the bow and arrow. The latter was the first device capable of storing energy for release when desired. These implements increased the range and striking force of primitive hunters and enabled them to slaughter the largest and fleetest animals.

All the basic hand tools in use today—the ax, adze, knife, drill, scraper, chisel, saw—were invented during the Stone Age. Bronze, the first metal, did not replace stone as the preferred material for tool making until about 3,500 years ago. Metal not only imparted a far more efficient and durable cutting edge to tools but enabled them to be resharpened instead of thrown away after becoming dulled.

During the period when bronze tools were the chief implements of production, means and standards of measurements were devised; mathematics and surveying were developed; a calendar was calculated; and great advances were made in sculpturing. Such basic inventions as the potter's wheel, the balance scale, the keystone arch, sailing vessels, and glass bottles were created.

About 2,500 years ago, iron, the most durable, plentiful, and cheap metal, began to displace bronze in tool making. As they became dominant, iron tools tremendously advanced productivity and skills in agriculture and craftsmanship. They enabled more food to be grown and better clothing and shelter to be made with less expenditure of time and energy; they gave rise to many comforts and conveniences. Iron tools made possible many of the achievements of Greece and Rome, from the Acropolis of Athens to the tunnels, bridges, sewers, and buildings of Rome.

The energy for all these earlier means and modes of production was supplied exclusively by human muscle power, which, after the domestication of herds, was supplemented to some extent by animal muscle power. The Industrial Revolution of the eighteenth century was based upon the utilization of energy from other sources, from fossil fuels such as coal. The combination of mechanical power generated by steam engines, machine tools, improved implements, and production machinery, plus the increased use of iron and steel, have multiplied society's powers of production to their present point. Nowadays, machines and tools operated by mechanical and electrical power are the principal material organs of our industry and agriculture alike.

The most up-to-date machine tools have been developed out of simple hand tools. While using hand tools, men began to understand and employ the advantages of the lever, the pulley, the inclined plane, the wheel and axle, and the screw to multiply their strength. These physical principles were later combined and applied in the making of machine tools.

This entire development of technology is organically associated with and primarily responsible for the development of mankind's intellectual abilities. This is pointed out in the following explanatory paragraph from the DoAll Corporation exhibit:

> Machine tools perform in complicated ways the same basic functions and operations as hand tools. These basic functions were established by hand-held stone tools shaped by primitive man. It was through devising and using hand-wrought stone tools that mankind developed powers of mental and bodily coordination . . . and this in turn accelerated the increase in men's mental capabilities.

Such ideas about the influence of technology upon thought, taken from the publication of a respectable capitalist corporation, resemble those to be found in the writings of Marx and Engels. The thought-controllers may try to drive historical materialism out of the socialist door, but here it sneaks back in through a capitalist window.

∾

The DoAll exhibit demonstrates that the evolution of tools arranged chronologically has an ascending order, from wood and stone hand tools through metal hand tools to power-driven machine tools. Is it likewise possible to mark off corresponding successive stages in social organization?

Historical materialism answers this question affirmatively. On the broadest basis—and every big division of history can be broken down for special purposes into lesser ones—three main stages can be distinguished in man's rise from animality to the present. Since the founding of anthropological studies in the mid-1800s, the three have commonly been known as: savagery, barbarism, and civilization.

It has been said that an army marches on its stomach. This has been true of the forward march of the army of humanity. The acquisition of food has been the overriding aim of social production at all times, for men cannot survive, let alone progress, without regularly satisfying their hunger.

The principal epochs in the advancement of humanity can therefore be divided according to the decisive improvements effected in securing food supplies.

Savagery, the infancy of humanity, constitutes that period when people depend for food upon what nature provides ready-made. Their food may come from plants, such as fruit or roots, from insects, birds or animals, or from seashore or sea life. At this stage, men forage for their food much like beasts of prey or grub for it like other animals—with these all-important differences: they cooperate with one another, and they employ crude tools along with other means and powers of production to assist them in "appropriating" the means of subsistence for their collective use.

The chief economic activities at this stage are foraging for food, hunting, and fishing; and they were developed in that sequence. The club and spear enable the savage to capture the raw materials for his meals, clothing, and shelter—all of which are embodied in animals on the hoof. The net catches fish and the fire prepares it for consumption. The indigenous peoples of southern California were at this stage when the first European settlers arrived in the 1760s.

Barbarism is the second stage of social organization. It was based upon the domestication of animals and the

Women, social labor, and the birth of civilization

Women acquired their leading place in primitive society not simply because they were the procreators of new life, but because, as a result of this particular function, they became the primordial producers of the necessities of life. At a certain point in the struggle to survive and to feed and care for their offspring, they took to the road of labor activities, and this new function made them the founders and leaders of the earliest form of social life.

We can cite the vast range of productive activities of primitive women and the crucial part they played in elevating mankind out of the lowly savage economy. During the period when men were occupied as full-time hunters, women developed most of the basic tools, skills, and techniques at the base of social advancement.

From food collecting they moved on to simple horticulture and then to agriculture. Out of the great variety of crafts they practiced, which included pot making, leather making, textile making, house building, etc., they developed the rudiments of botany, chemistry, medicine, and other branches of scientific knowledge.

As Engels demonstrated, it was through productive activities that mankind arose out of the animal world. More concretely, then, it was the female half of humanity who initiated these productive activities and who must therefore be credited with the major share in this great act of creation and elevation of humanity.

EVELYN REED, 1969
Problems of Women's Liberation

cultivation of plants. Food is now not merely *collected* but *produced*. The domestication of cattle, sheep, pigs, and other animals provided reserves of meat as well as food in the form of milk from goats and cows. The planting and growing of crops made regular and plentiful food supplies available.

This food-producing revolution, which started in Asia around ten thousand years ago, relieved mankind from subjection to external nature for the first time. Up to that point humanity had had to rely upon what the natural environment contained to take care of its needs and had been dependent for survival upon completely external and uncontrollable natural conditions. Entire stocks and cultures of people arose, flourished, and then succumbed, like plant or animal species, in response to the beneficence or hostility of nature around them.

For example, about twenty to thirty thousand years ago, there arose a society centered around southern France called the Reindeer Culture. These people thrived by hunting huge reindeer and other herds that browsed upon the lush vegetation there. The drawings they made, first discovered in caves in the nineteenth century, testify to the keenness of their eyes and minds and the trained sensitivity of their hands and place them among the most superb artists that have ever appeared on earth. However, when changed climatic and botanical conditions caused the reindeer herds to vanish, their entire culture, and very likely the people as well, died out.

The early hunters had no assured control over their mobile sources of food. The insecurity of life was largely overcome, or at least considerably reduced, with the advent of stockbreeding, and especially with the development of agricultural techniques. For the first time, methods were instituted for obtaining extensive and expanding supplies of food products and fibers by systematic and sustained activities of working groups. These branches of economic activity made much larger and more compact populations possible.

These activities and their increased output provided the elements for the higher culture of barbarism. Farming and stock raising led to the development of such handicrafts as smelting and pottery, as accumulated food supplies generated the need to store and transport articles for the first time. Human beings became more stationary; denser populations aggregated; permanent dwellings were built; and village life sprang into existence.

In their further and final development, the economic activities under barbarism created the prerequisites for the coming of civilization. The material foundation for civilization was the capacity acquired by the most advanced peoples for the regular production of far more food and goods than were required for the physical maintenance of their members.

These surpluses had two results. They permitted specific sections of the communities to engage in diversified activities other than the direct acquisition and production of the basic means of life. Along with priests, nobles, kings, and officials, specialists such as traders, builders, smiths, potters, and other craftsmen made their appearance.

With the growth of specialization and the extension of trade, the top layers of these groups moved into strategic positions that enabled the more fortunate and powerful to appropriate large personal shares of the surplus of wealth. The drive to increase personal wealth flowing from the growing social division of labor and exchange of goods, led in time to the development of private property, the family, slavery, class divisions, commodity production on a large scale, trade, money, the city, and the territorial state with its army, police, courts, and other relations and institutions characteristic of civilization.

∼

In its evolution to our own century, civilized society can be divided into three main epochs: slavery, feudalism, and capitalism. Each of these is marked off by the special way in which the ruling propertied class at the head of the social setup manages to extract the surplus wealth upon which it lives from the laboring mass who directly create it. This entire period covers little more than the past five to six thousand years.

Civilization was ushered in and raised upon direct slavery. The very economic factors that broke up barbarism and made civilized life possible likewise provided the material preconditions for the use of slave labor. The division of labor based upon tending herds, raising crops, mining metals, and fashioning goods for sale enabled the most advanced societies to produce more than the actual laborers required for their maintenance.

This made slavery both possible and profitable for the first time. It gave the most powerful stimulus to the predatory appetites of individual possessors of the means of production who strove to acquire and increase their surpluses of wealth. Slave production and ownership became the economic foundation of a new type of social organization, the source of supreme power, prestige, and privileges. And it eventually reshaped the whole structure of civilized life

Chattel slavery was an extremely significant human contrivance—and it is distinctively human. Animals may feed upon carcasses of other animals, but they do not live upon the surpluses they create. Although we rightly recoil against any manifestations of servitude today and burn to

Class society can be divided into three main epochs: slavery, feudalism, and capitalism. Each is defined by the dominant form of production the propertied class uses to extract surplus wealth from the laboring masses.

For most of its existence, human society was based on bare subsistence and shared labor. There were no social classes, no repressive state powers. Beginning some 5,000 years ago, the capacity to produce a food surplus led to the emergence of private property and of social classes with conflicting interests—the propertyless producers versus the propertied rulers.

Above: Slaves in ancient Greece unloading merchant ship.

Below: Serfs harvesting wheat in feudal England, early 14th century.

abolish its last vestiges, it should be recognized that in its heyday slavery had imperative reasons for existence and persistence.

Science demands that every phenomenon be approached, analyzed, and appraised with objectivity, setting aside personal reactions of admiration or abhorrence. Historical materialism has to explain why slavery came to be adopted by the most advanced contingents of mankind.

The principal reason was that, along with the private ownership of the means of production and the widening exchange of its products, slave labor increased the forces of production, multiplied wealth, comforts and culture—although only for the lucky few—and, on the whole, spurred mankind forward for an entire historical period. Without the extension of slave labor, there would not have been incentives unremitting enough to pile up wealth on a sizable scale that could then be applied to further the productive processes.

The historical necessity for slavery can be illustrated along two lines. The peoples who failed to adopt slave labor likewise did not proceed to civilization, however excellent their other qualities and deeds. They remained below that level because their economy lacked the inner drive of the force of greed and the dynamic propulsion arising from the slaveholder's need to exploit the slave to augment his wealth. That is a negative demonstration.

But there is more positive proof. Those states based on some form of servitude, such as the most brilliant cultures of antiquity from Babylon and Egypt to Greece and Rome, also contributed the most to the civilizing processes, from wheeled carts and the plow to writing and philosophy. These societies stood in the main line of social progress.

But if slavery had sufficient reasons for becoming the beginning and basis of ancient civilization, in turn and in

'Trotsky taught me to be a citizen of the world'

The following is from Farrell Dobbs's testimony at the 1981 trial in the Socialist Workers Party lawsuit exposing decades of FBI spying and disruption against the party and other political organizations. Dobbs, a central leader of the 1930s Teamster unionization battles in the Midwest, was Socialist Workers Party national secretary from 1953 to 1972. Here he describes the education in materialist dialectics he received during a 1940 discussion in Mexico with Russian revolutionary leader Leon Trotsky.

Trotsky was very perspicacious about what I needed. He taught me not to be provincial in contemporary times but to be a citizen of the world.

He talked about the main stages of the evolution of social organization in history—slave, feudal, capitalist, and so on—and how each of these at their inception had progressive features. They served, within limits, to advance humanity's striving to improve its technology and derive a better living from the natural resources of the earth. But as progress was made, each system came to serve as a barrier to further advance.

I said to him I can understand that except for one thing. I can't conceive how there could be anything progressive about slavery.

He called to my attention that prior to the advent of the slave system, which marked a leap in the development of agricultural production, it had been the habit of warring tribes to eat their captives. He said, "It is, after

all, infinitely more progressive to be a slave in the field
than to be a roast on the dinner table."

I began to see then what he meant about the importance of understanding what conditions were like at
each stage of this long evolution of history.

APRIL 2, 1981
FBI on Trial

time it generated the conditions and forces which would
undermine and overthrow it. Once slavery became the
predominant form of production either in industry, as
in Greece, or in agriculture, as in Rome, it no longer fur-
thered the development of agricultural techniques, craftsmanship, trade, or navigation. The slave empires of antiquity stagnated and disintegrated until after a lapse of
centuries they were replaced by two main types of feudal
organization: Asiatic and West European.

As the result of a long list of technological and other
social advances, merging with a sequence of exceptional
historical circumstances, feudalized Europe became the
nursery for the next great stage of class society, capitalism.
How and why did capitalism originate?

Once money had arisen from the extension of trad-
ing several thousand years ago, its use as capital became
possible. Merchants could add to their wealth by buying
goods cheap and selling them dear; moneylenders and
mortgage holders could gain interest on sums advanced
on the security of land or other collateral. These practices
were common in both slave and feudal societies.

But if money could be used in precapitalist times to return
more than the original investment, other conditions had to
be fulfilled before capitalism could become established as a

separate and definite world economic system. The central condition was a special kind of transaction regularly repeated on a growing scale. Large numbers of propertyless workers had to hire themselves to the possessors of money and the other means of production in order to earn a livelihood.

Hiring and firing seem to us a normal way of carrying on production. But peoples such as the indigenous North Americans never knew it. Before the Europeans came, no Indian ever worked for a boss (the word itself was imported by the Dutch), because they possessed their own means of livelihood. The slave may have been purchased, but he belonged to and worked for the master his whole life long. The feudal serf or tenant was likewise bound for life to the lord and his land.

> **The epoch-making innovation upon which capitalism rested was the vast expansion of working for wages as the dominant relation of production.**

The epoch-making innovation upon which capitalism rested was the vast expansion of working for wages as the dominant relation of production. Most of you have gone into the labor market, to an employment agency or personnel office, to get a buyer for your labor power. The employer buys this power at prevailing wage rates by the hour, day, or week and then applies it under his supervision to produce commodities that his company subsequently sells at a profit. That profit is derived from the fact that wage workers produce more value than the capitalist pays for their labor power.

Up to the twentieth century, this mechanism for pumping surplus labor out of the working masses and transferring the surpluses of wealth they create to the personal credit of the capitalist was the mightiest accelerator of the productive forces and the expansion of civilization.

As a distinct economic system, capitalism only dates back to the early 1500s; it has conquered the world and journeyed from dawn to twilight in that time. This is a short life span compared to savagery, which stretched over a million years or more, or to barbarism, which prevailed for four thousand to five thousand years. Obviously, the processes of social transformation have been considerably speeded up in modern times.

This acceleration of social progress is due in large measure to the very nature of capitalism, which continually revolutionizes its techniques of production and the entire range of social relations issuing from them. Since its birth, world capitalism has passed through three such phases of internal transformation. In its formative period, the merchants were the dominant class of capitalists because trade was the main source of wealth accumulation. Under commercial capitalism, industry and agriculture, the pillars of production, were not usually carried on by wage labor but by means of small handicrafts, peasant farming, slave or serf labor.

The industrial age was launched around the beginning of the nineteenth century with the application of steam power to the first mechanized processes, concentrating large numbers of wage workers into factories. The capitalist captains of this large-scale industry became masters of the field of production and later of entire countries and continents as their riches, their legions of wage laborers, social and political power, swelled to majestic proportions.

This vigorous, expanding, progressive, confident, competitive stage of industrial capitalism dominated the nineteenth century. It passed over into the monopoly-ridden capitalism of the twentieth century, which has carried all the basic tendencies of capitalism, and especially its most reactionary features, to extremes in economic, political, cultural, and international relations.

While the processes of production have become more centralized, more rationalized, more socialized, the means of production and the wealth of the world have become concentrated in giant financial and industrial combines. So far as the capitalist sectors of society are involved, this process has been brought to the point where the capitalist monopolies of a single country, the US, largely dictate to all the rest.

~

The most important question to be asked at this point is: What is the destiny of the development of civilization in its capitalist form? Disregarding in-between views, which at bottom evade the answer, two irreconcilable viewpoints assert themselves, corresponding to the world outlooks of two opposing classes.

The spokesmen for capitalism say that nothing more remains to be done except to perfect their system as it stands, and it can roll on and on and on. The DoAll Corporation, for example, which published so instructive a chart on the evolution of tools, declares that more and better machine tools, which they hope will be bought at substantial profit from their company, will guarantee continued progress and prosperity for capitalist America without the least change in existing class relations.

Socialists give a completely different answer based upon an incomparably more penetrating, correct, and comprehensive analysis of the movement of history, the structure of capitalism, and the struggles presently agitating the world around us. The historical function of capitalism is not to perpetuate itself indefinitely but to create the conditions and prepare the forces that will bring about its own replacement by a more efficient form of material production and a higher type of social organization.

Just as capitalism supplanted feudalism and slavery, and civilization swept aside savagery and barbarism, so the time has come for capitalism itself to be superseded. How and by whom is this revolutionary transformation to be effected?

In the nineteenth century, Marx made a scientific analysis of the workings of the capitalist system which explained how its inner contradictions would bring about its downfall. The revolutions since 1917 are demonstrating in real life that capitalism is due to be relegated to the museum of antiquities. It is worthwhile to understand the inexorable underlying causes of these developments, which appear so inexplicable and abhorrent to the upholders of the capitalist system.

Capitalism has produced many things, good and bad, in the course of its evolution. But the most vital and valuable of all the social forces it has created is the industrial working class. The capitalist class has brought into existence a vast army of wage laborers, centralized and disciplined, and set it into motion for its own purposes, to make and operate the machines, factories, and all the other production and transportation facilities from which its profits emanate.

The exploitation and abuses, inherent and inescapable in the capitalist organization of economic life, provoke the workers time and again to organize themselves and undertake militant action to defend their elementary

Capitalism has produced many things, good and bad, in the course of its evolution. The most vital of all the social forces it has created is the working class.

Workers at Putilov locomotive factory in Petrograd, Russia, meet in July 1920 to elect deputies to city's soviet (council), local body of the new revolutionary workers and peasants government.

In October 1917, working people in the former Russian Empire overturned the rule of capitalists and landlords and took state power. Led by the Bolshevik Party, they launched a socialist revolution that began to transform economic and social relations in the interests of the vast majority.

interests. The struggle between these conflicting social classes is today the dominant and driving force of world and American history, just as the conflict between the bourgeois-led forces against the precapitalist elements was the motivating force of history in the immediately preceding centuries.

The current struggle, which has been gathering momentum and expanding its scope since the middle of the 1800s, has entered its decisive phase on a world scale.

The greatest preliminary battles to establish an economic and social order free of exploitation, compulsion, and the private expropriation of the fruits of our labor—a socialist world order—have so far been waged in countries outside the Western Hemisphere.

Sooner or later, however, they are bound to break out and be fought to a finish within this country, which is not only the stronghold of capitalist power but also the home of the best-organized and technically most proficient working class on this globe.

The main line of development in America, no less than the course of world history, points to such a conclusion. Why is this so?

The main course of US history

George Novack

We have reviewed the course by which humanity climbed out of the animal state, and we have marked the successive steps in that climb. Mankind had to crawl through savagery for a million years or more, walk through barbarism, and then, with shoulders hunched and head bowed, enter the iron gates of class society.

There, for thousands of years, mankind has endured a harsh schooling under the rod and rule of private property, which began with slavery and reached its highest form in capitalist civilization. Now our own age stands, or rather struggles, at the entrance to socialism.

Let us now pass from the historical progress of mankind, viewed as a whole, to inspect one of its parts, the United States of North America. Because US imperialism is the mainstay of the international capitalist system, the role of

---

The second of two talks given in September 1955 at the Socialist Workers Party's West Coast school and camp, held near Los Angeles, California.

the American people is crucial in deciding how quickly and how well humanity crosses the great divide between the class society of the past and the reorganization and reinvigoration of the world along socialist lines.

I shall try to give brief answers to the following four questions: What has been the course of American history in its essentials? What are its connections with the march of the rest of humankind? What has been the outcome to date? Finally, where do we fit into the picture?

~

American history breaks sharply into two fundamentally different epochs. One belongs to the aboriginal inhabitants, the Indians. The other starts with the coming of Europeans to America at the end of the fifteenth century.

The beginnings of human activity in the Western Hemisphere are still obscure. But it is surmised that from twenty to thirty thousand years ago, early Stone Age Asians, thanks to favorable climatic conditions that united Alaska with Siberia, crossed over the Bering Strait and slowly made their way throughout North, Central, and South America. Over millennia the first human inhabitants of the Americas fashioned their existence.

Whoever regards the Indians as insignificant or incompetent has defective historical judgment. Humanity has been raised to its present estate by four branches of productive activity. The first is food gathering, which includes grubbing for roots and berries as well as hunting and fishing. The second is stock raising. The third is agriculture. The fourth is craftsmanship, graduating into large-scale industry.

The Indians were extremely adept at hunting, fishing, and other ways of food gathering. They were ingenious craftsmen whose work in some fields has never been excelled. The Incas, for example, made textiles that were extremely fine in texture, coloring, and design. They invented and used more different techniques of weaving on their handlooms than any other people in history.

However, the Indians showed the greatest talent in their development of agriculture. They may have independently invented soil cultivation. In any case they brought it to diversified perfection. We are indebted to American Indians for most of the vegetables that today come from the fields and through the kitchens onto our tables. Most important are corn, potatoes, and beans, but there is in addition a considerable list including tomatoes, chili peppers, pineapples, peanuts, avocados, and tobacco.

They knew and used the properties of four hundred separate species of plants. No plant cultivated by the American Indians was known to Asia, Europe, or Africa prior to the European invasion of America.

Much is heard about all that the Europeans brought over to the Indians, but little about what the Indians gave the Europeans. The introduction of the food plants taken from the Indians more than doubled the available food supply of the older continent after the fifteenth century and became an important factor in the expansion of capitalist civilization. Over half of the agricultural produce raised in the world today comes from plants domesticated by the Indians!

From the first to the fifteenth centuries, the Indians themselves created magnificent, even astounding cultures on the basis of their achievements in agriculture. Agriculture enabled some of the scattered and roving hunting tribes to aggregate in small but permanent settlements where they supported themselves by growing corn, beans, and other vegetables. They also raised and wove cotton, made pottery, and developed other handicrafts.

'Columbus discovered the road to the world'

From remarks by Armando Hart, a central leader of the Cuban Revolution and longtime minister of culture. Hart addressed an October 1992 event in Holguín, Cuba, that marked the 500th anniversary of Christopher Columbus's arrival in the Americas.

This is an event worthy of celebrating. Like all great events, it was fraught with contradictions. But no one can deny that it opened a new era in human history.

Columbus did not discover a "new world"—it had already existed since our earliest ancestors arrived through the Bering Strait in what is now the Americas.

Before 1492 there was no world in the modern sense. What was called the world was only a fragment of the Earth.

Columbus deserves our respect, deserves to be remembered, because what he really discovered five centuries ago was the road to the world. That discovery was even greater than what the Admiral imagined he had found.

At the same time, this action also led to the conquest, to the extermination of the native population and the expansion of slavery. It led to the growth of capitalism in a vast part of the world.

Besides Christopher Columbus, we must remember the figure of the Indian chief Hatuey, who came from Santo Domingo to fight the conquerors and died in eastern Cuba. In the resistance to the effects of the conquest we also find father Bartolomé de las Casas. This resistance eventually led to the independence movements in the Americas and to liberation from the yoke of the European powers.

The Incas of the Andes, the Mayans of Guatemala and Yucatán, and the Aztecs of central Mexico, unaffected by European civilization and having developed independently, constituted the most advanced of the Indian societies. Their cultures embodied the utmost the Indians were able to accomplish within the twenty-five thousand years or so allotted them by history. In fact, the Mayans had made mathematical and astronomical calculations more complex and advanced than those of the European invaders. They had independently invented the zero for use in their number system—something even the Greeks and Romans had lacked.

Indians progressed as far as the middle stage of barbarism and were stopped there. Whether or not, given unlimited time and no interference from more powerful and productive peoples, they would have risen all the way to civilization must remain unanswered.

This much can be stated: they had formidable obstacles to overcome along such a path. The Indians did not have such important domesticated animals as the horse, cow, pig, sheep, or water buffalo that had pulled the Asians and Europeans along toward civilization. They had only the dog, turkey, guinea pig, and, in the Andean highlands, llamas, alpacas, and, in some places, bees. Moreover, they did not use the wheel, except for toys, did not know the use of iron or firearms, and did not have other prerequisites for a level of productivity sufficient to give rise to private property.

However, history in the other part of the globe settled this question without further appeal. For, while the most advanced Indians had been moving up from wandering hunters' lives to those settled in communities, the Europeans, themselves an offspring of Asiatic culture, had not only entered class society but their most progressive segments along the Atlantic seaboard were passing over from feudalism to capitalism.

This uneven development of society in the Old World and the New provided the historical setting for the second great turning point in the history of the Americas. What was the essential meaning of the upheaval initiated by the West European crossing of the Atlantic? It represented the transition from the Stone Age to the Iron Age in America, from barbaric to civilized modes of life, from tribal organization based upon collectivist practices to a society rooted in private property, production for exchange, the family, the state, and so forth.

Few spectacles in history are more dramatic and instructive than the confrontation and conflict between the Indian representatives of communal Stone Age life and the armed agents of class civilization. Science fiction tells about visitations to this planet by Martians in flying saucers. To the Indians, the first visitations of the white-skinned Europeans were no less startling and incomprehensible.

To the Indians, these men had completely alien customs, standards, and ways of life. They were strange in appearance and behavior. In fact, the differences between the two were so profound as to be irreconcilable. What was the root cause of the prolonged and deadly clash between them? They represented two utterly incompatible levels of social organization that had grown out of and were based upon dissimilar conditions and were heading toward entirely different goals.

"Columbus's arrival in America, like all major events, was fraught with contradictions. But no one can deny it opened a new era in human history. Before 1492 there was no world in the modern sense."

—*Armando Hart, 1992*

At an event marking 500 years since Columbus's landing on Cuban shores, Armando Hart, Cuba's minister of culture, also paid tribute to those who fought the plunder and extermination of the native peoples of the Caribbean and Latin America.

Hart singled out Hatuey, the Taíno chief who led resistance to the Spanish conquerors and was burned at the stake in Cuba, and Bartolomé de las Casas, the 16th century Spanish priest who denounced the genocide of the indigenous population.

Above, left: "Hatuey, first rebel in the Americas," reads plaque on monument in Baracoa, Cuba. **Above, right:** Bartolomé de las Casas, in 18th century portrait.

Even at its height, Indian life was based upon tribal collectivism and its crude technology. Indian psychology was fashioned by such social institutions. The Indians not only did not have the wheel, iron, or the alphabet—they also lacked the institutions, ideas, feelings, and aims of peoples who had been molded over millennia by the technology and culture of an acquisitive society. These conditions had stamped out a very special kind of human being as the peculiar product of civilization based upon private ownership.

The most highly developed Indians subsisted on agriculture. But their agriculture was not of the same economic mode as that of the newcomers. The major means of producing food by soil cultivation belonged to the entire tribe and nothing in its production or distribution could be exclusively claimed by individual owners. This was true of the principal means of production, the land itself. When the Europeans arrived at these shores, all the way from the Atlantic to the Pacific there was not a single foot of ground about which someone could assert: "This belongs to me, my solitary private self, or to my little family—all others keep off and stay out." The land belonged to the whole people.

It was quite otherwise with the Europeans, the bearers of the new and higher stage of society. To them it appeared natural and necessary, as it still does to most citizens of this country, that almost everything on earth should pass into someone's private ownership. Clothes, houses, weapons of war, tools, ships, even human beings themselves, could be bought and sold.

It was in the shiny embodiment of precious metals that private property became not only the cornerstone of worldly existence but even opened up the gates of heaven. Christopher Columbus wrote to Spain's Queen Isabella as follows: "Gold constitutes treasure and he who possesses it has all he needs in this world as also the means of rescuing souls from purgatory and restoring them to the enjoyment of paradise." This was literally true at that time because rich Catholics could buy indulgences for their sins from the Pope. Conquistador Hernán Cortés is said to have told some natives of Mexico: "We Spaniards are troubled with a disease of the heart for which we find gold, and gold only, a specific remedy."

In their quest for gold and lust for gain, the conquistadors enslaved and killed hundreds of thousands of indigenous Americans.

The doctrine of the Europeans was that everything must have its price, whether it pertains to present happiness or future salvation. This idea remains the guideline for the plutocratic rulers of our own day, who in their campaigns to dominate the world not only buy up individuals but even whole governments. In their quest for gold and lust for gain, Columbus and the conquistadors enslaved and killed thousands of indigenous Americans in the islands they discovered. And that was only the beginning.

Viewed from the heights of world history, this turning point in America was characterized by the conjuncture of two revolutionary processes. The first was the shift of maritime Europe from a feudal to a bourgeois society. Part of this revolutionizing of Western Europe was a push outward as the capitalist traders extended their operations throughout the globe. Their exploring, marketing, pirating expeditions brought the emissaries of the budding bour-

A collision of two levels
of socio-economic development

The three-century-long war between the indigenous peoples of North America and the European aggressors involved the collision of two disparate levels of historical development, two fundamentally different socio-economic formations, two irreconcilable modes of life, types of culture, and outlooks upon the world.

The defeat of the native tribes was predetermined by the incomparably greater powers of production and destruction, numbers, wealth, and organization on the side of the classes composing bourgeois civilization.

GEORGE NOVACK, 1970
Genocide against the Indians:
Its Role in the Rise of U.S. Capitalism

geois society in Europe across the ocean and into collision with the native tribes. The rape of the ancient cultures of the Aztecs and Incas, the enslavement and extermination of the natives by the Spanish conquerors and others, was a collateral offensive of this European revolution on our own continent.

Through the extension of the revolutionary process, the peoples of the Stone Age here were overcome and supplanted by the most advanced representatives of class civilization. This was not the only continent on which such a process took place. What happened from the fifteenth to the nineteenth centuries in the New World had taken place much earlier in Western Europe itself; and it was to reach into the most remote sectors of the world, as capitalism has spread over the earth from that time to our own.

The contest between the Stone Age peoples and the representatives of the bourgeois epoch was fiercely fought. Their wars across the Americas stretched over four centuries and ended in the disintegration, dispossession, or destruction of the prehistoric cultures and the unchallenged supremacy of class society.

With the advent of the Europeans, along with the enslaved Africans who were transported here by them, American history was switched onto an entirely different set of rails, a new course marked out by the needs of a young, expanding world capitalism.

∾

We come now to a most crucial question: What has been the main line of American growth since 1492? Various answers are given—the growth of national independence, the spread of democracy, the coming into his own of the common man, or the expansion of industry. Each of these familiar formulas taught in the schools does record some aspect of the process, but none goes to the heart of the matter.

The correct answer to the question is that despite detours en route, the main line of American history has consisted in the construction and consolidation of capitalist civilization, which has been carried to its ultimate point in our own day. Any attempt to explain the development of American society since the sixteenth century will be brought up against this fact.

The discovery, exploration, settlement, cultivation, exploitation, democratization, and industrialization of this continent must all be seen as successive steps in promoting the building of bourgeois society. This is the only interpretation of the decisive events in the past five centuries in North America that makes sense, that gives continu-

When Europeans arrived in the Americas, there was not a foot of ground a person could stand on and assert: "This belongs to me, to my solitary private self."

Sioux hunters pursue buffalo on North America's Great Plains, 1830s, depicted by US painter George Catlin.

Europeans arriving in North America brought with them economic and social relations incompatible with the pre-class organization of the indigenous peoples. Over three centuries, wars of extermination put an end to "tribal organization based upon collectivist practices and led to a class-divided society rooted in private property, production for exchange, the family, and the state." Capitalism in the United States was consolidated.

ity and coherence to our complex history, distinguishes the main stream from tributaries, and is validated by the development of American society. Everything in our national history has to be referred to, and linked up with, the process of establishing the capitalist way of life in its most pronounced and, today, its most pernicious form.

This is sometimes called the "American way of life." A more realistic and honest characterization would be the capitalist way of life because, as I shall indicate, this is destined to be only a historically limited and passing expression of civilized life in America.

The central importance of the formation and transformation of bourgeois society can be demonstrated in another way. What is the most outstanding peculiarity of American history since the coming of the Europeans?

There have been many peculiarities in the history of this country; in some ways this is a very peculiar country. But what marks off American life from the development of the other great nations of the world is that the growth and construction of American society falls entirely within the epoch of the expansion of capitalism on a global scale. That is the key to understanding American history, whether you deal with colonial history, nineteenth-century history, or twentieth-century history.

It is not true of other major countries such as England, Germany, Russia, India, Japan, or China. These countries passed through prolonged periods of slave or feudal civilization that left their stamp upon them to this very day. Look at US general Douglas MacArthur's preservation of that feudal relic, the emperor of Japan, in the aftermath of World War II, or that Sunday newspaper supplement delight, the monarchy of England.

America, on the other hand, leaped from savagery and barbarism to capitalism, tipping its hat along the way to slavery and feudalism, which held no more than subordinate places in building the bourgeois system. In a couple of centuries, the American people hurried through stages of social development that took the rest of mankind many thousands of years. But there was close interconnection between these two processes. If the rest of mankind had not already made these acquisitions, we Americans would not have been able to rush ahead so far and so fast. The tasks of pioneers are invariably harder and take far longer to accomplish.

The fusion of the antifeudal revolution in Europe with the wars of extermination against the Indians ushered in the bourgeois epoch of American history. This period has stretched over five centuries. It falls into three distinct phases, each marked off by revolutionary changes in American life.

$\sim$

The first period is that of colonial America, which extended from 1500 to the ratification of the US Constitution in 1787–89. If we analyze the social forms and economic forces of American life during these three centuries, colonial America, the formative period of our civilization, stands out as an exceptional blending of precapitalist agencies with the oncoming capitalist forms and forces of production.

The tribal collectivism of the Indians was being transformed, pushed back, annihilated; remnants of feudalism were imported from Europe and transplanted here. The *ranchos* of southern California in the early nineteenth century had been preceded by colonial baronies; entire colonies such as Maryland and Pennsylvania were owned by landed proprietors who had been given title to them by the English monarchy. Big planters exploited white indentured servants and African chattel slaves, who in many places provided the main labor forces.

Alongside them were hundreds of thousands of small farmers, hunters, trappers, artisans, traders, merchants, and others associated with the new forms of ownership and economic activity and animated by customs, feelings, and ideas stemming from the capitalism which was advancing in Europe and now beginning to flourish on this side of the Atlantic.

In colonial America, the fundamental question posed was which forces would prevail—precapitalist or capitalist?

The fundamental question posed by this development was—which would prevail, the precapitalist or the capitalist forces? This was the axis of the social struggles within the colonies and even of the incessant wars for possession of the New World among the European nations, which characterized the colonial period. The showdown on this front came in the years between 1763 and 1789, the period of the preparation, outbreak, waging, and conclusion of the First American Revolution. This was the first stage of the bourgeois-democratic revolution on this continent.

It assumed the form of a war between the rulers and supporters of Great Britain and the colonial masses led by representatives of the Northern merchants, bankers, and manufacturers, and of the planters of the Southern slave system, which was an appendage of growing native capitalism. The outcome of the contest determined the next stage in the destiny of American capitalism. If Great Britain's domination had persisted, that might have stunted and perverted the further development of bourgeois society here as it did in India and Africa.

The First American Revolution and its war for independence was a genuine people's movement. Such movements destroy much that has become rotten and is ready for burial. But, above all, they are socially creative, giving birth to institutions that provide the ways and means for the next surge forward. That was certainly true of our first national revolution, which is permanently embedded in the American and international consciousness. So powerful and persistent are its traditions that they are today a source of embarrassment to the capitalist rulers of this country in their dealings with current colonial movements for emancipation.

What were the notable achievements of this first stage of the North American bourgeois-democratic revolution?

It overthrew the reactionary rule of the ten thousand merchants, bankers, landowners, and manufacturers of Great Britain, who, after helping to spur the American colonies forward, had become the biggest block to their further advance. It brought independence to the colonies, unified them, and cleared away such feudal vestiges as the crown lands, which the monarchy held. It democratized the states and gave them a republican form of government. It cleared the ground for a swift expansion of civilization in its native capitalist forms from the Atlantic to the Pacific.

The revolution had international repercussions. It inspired and protected similar movements during the next century in the Latin American colonies and even radiated back to the Old Continent. Read the diary of Gouverneur Morris, a financial leader of the Patriot Party, who became one of the early US ambassadors to France in 1792.

The first stage of the American bourgeois-democratic revolution overthrew the reactionary rule of the British monarchy.

Revolt in Boston in 1765 against the British monarchy's hated Stamp Tax. Mechanics, longshoremen, sailors, and artisans, with the support of small farmers, were in the vanguard. "No taxation without representation!" was their cry.

When ten years of such resistance exploded into a popular revolutionary war, the colonial masses won independence in 1783 and established a republic. An alliance of Northern merchants, bankers, and manufacturers, together with Southern plantation slave owners, formed the new government.

He was in Paris selling American properties to aristocrats who were threatened with exile by the French Revolution. These clients complained to the sympathetic Morris that if only his countrymen had refrained from revolution, the French people would never have had the notion or courage to follow suit.

> **With the twin inventions of steam-driven machinery, notably in textiles, and the cotton gin, slavery acquired a new lease on life.**

But even the most thoroughgoing revolution cannot do more than historical possibilities permit. Two serious shortcomings in the work of this first upheaval manifested themselves in the next decades. One was the fact that the revolution did not and could not eliminate the soil in which the institution of slavery was rooted. Many leaders of the time, among them Thomas Jefferson, hoped that slavery would wither away because of unfavorable economic conditions.

The second shortcoming was that although the revolt gave Americans political independence, it could not give thoroughgoing independence to the US in a capitalist sense. This was true in two ways: at home the Northern capitalists had to share power with the Southern slave owners, with whom they had waged the revolutionary war for independence and set up the new government; on the international market they remained in economic subordination to the more advanced industrial and financial structure of England.

The leaders of the revolution were aware of these deficiencies. The same Gouverneur Morris wrote to President George Washington from Paris on September 30, 1791:

> We shall . . . make great and rapid progress in useful manufactures. This alone is wanting to complete our independence. We shall then be as it were a world by ourselves, and far from the jars and wars of Europe, their various revolutions will serve merely to instruct and amuse. Like the roaring of a tempestuous sea, which at a certain distance becomes a pleasing sound.

However, a historical freak came along, which upset this pleasant prospect. This freak was the result of a double revolution in technology, one which took place in Europe, especially in English industry, and the other in American agriculture. The establishment of factories with steam-driven machinery in English industry, notably in textiles, its most important branch, created the demand for large supplies of cotton. The invention of the cotton gin enabled the Southern planters to supply that demand.

Consequently, slavery, which had been withering on the vine, acquired a new lease on life. This economic combination invested the nobles of the Southern cotton kingdom with tremendous wealth and power. A study of American history in the first half of the nineteenth century shows that its national and political life was dominated and directed by the struggle for supremacy waged by the forces centered around the Southern slaveholders on one side and those of the antislavery elements on the other.

The crucial social issue before the nation was not always stated bluntly. But when every other conflict was traced to its roots, it was found to be connected with the question: What are we Americans going to do about slavery?

Slavery in the US was driven by capitalism, not vice versa

The following are excerpts from two works by Karl Marx.

[In economies like the US South and Caribbean colonies based on] plantations, where commercial speculations figure from the start and production is intended for the world market, capitalist production exists, although only in a formal sense, since the slavery of Negroes precludes free wage labor, which is the basis of capitalist production.

But the business in which slaves are used is conducted by *capitalists*. The mode of production which they introduce has not arisen out of slavery but is grafted onto it. In this case, the same person is capitalist and landowner.

Theories of Surplus Value, 1861–63

The fact that we now not only describe the plantation owners in America as capitalists, but that they *are* capitalists, is due to the fact that they exist as anomalies within a world market based upon free labor.

Economic Manuscripts of 1857–58 (Grundrisse)

(A similar situation exists today in relation to capitalism. No matter what dispute agitates the political-economic life of this country, it sooner or later brings up the great social-economic question: What are we Americans going to do about capitalism?)

For the first fifty years of the nineteenth century, the cotton aristocrats of the South undeniably held center stage.

They became very cocky about their power and privileges, which they thought would last indefinitely. Then, around 1850, conditions began to change quite rapidly. A new combination of social forces appeared that was to prove strong enough not only to challenge the slave power but to meet it in civil war, conquer and eliminate it.

It is highly instructive to study the mentality and outlook of the American people in 1848. That was a year of revolutions in the principal countries of Western Europe. The people in the United States, including its governing groups, viewed these outbursts in an isolationist spirit.

The European revolutions even pleased certain sections of the ruling classes in the United States because they were directed mainly against monarchies. There were no monarchies here to overthrow, although there was a slave aristocracy rooted in the South. Although most of the common people in the United States sympathized with the European revolutions, they looked upon them as no more than a catching up with what had already been achieved in this country. The Americans said to themselves: "We've already had our revolution and don't need any more here. The quota of revolutions assigned to us by history is exhausted."

They did not see even fifteen years into their own future. The bourgeois-democratic revolution still had considerable unfinished business. During the 1850s, it became plainer that the Southern slaveholders were not only tightening their autocracy in the Southern states but were trying to make slaves of the entire population of the United States. This small set of rich men arrogated to themselves the right to tell the people what they could and could not do, where the country should expand, and how the affairs of America should and should not be managed.

US political life in the first half of the 19th century was dominated by the struggle for supremacy between the slavocracy and the rising industrial bourgeoisie.

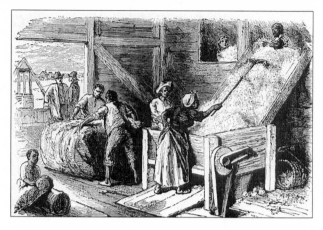

Above: Slaves working cotton gin on a Southern plantation.

Below: Port Richmond coal depot, Philadelphia, 1852. Coal from Pennsylvania mines was brought by canal and rail to this river port and shipped to New York, Boston, and other industrial centers.

Invention of the steam engine and cotton gin led to a massive expansion of slave-produced cotton in the mid-1800s, boosting the wealth and power of the slavocracy. As factory production employing free labor accelerated in the North, it led to the inevitable showdown between the slaveholding class and emerging industrial capitalist forces.

So a second revolution proved necessary to complete those tasks left unsettled in the late eighteenth century and to dispose of the main problems that had confronted the American people in the meantime. There had to be thirteen years of preparatory struggles, four and a half years of civil war, twelve years of Reconstruction—about thirty years in all, in this intense and inescapable revolutionary upheaval.

What is most important for us now are the net results of that travail. Every schoolchild knows that the slave power was abolished and the Negro population unshackled from chattel slavery. But the principal achievement of this revolution from the standpoint of American and world development was that the last of the internal impediments to the march of American capitalism were leveled, and the way cleared for the consolidation of capitalist rule.

That period saw the conclusion of the contest that had been going on since 1492 between the procapitalist and precapitalist forces on this continent. See what had happened to the peoples representing the diverse precapitalist ways of life.

The Indian tribes, whose level of productivity had not advanced beyond savagery and barbarism, had either been exterminated, dispossessed, or herded into reservations.

England, which had upheld feudalism and colonial subjugation, had been swept aside and American industrial capital had attained not only political supremacy but economic independence.

The Southern slavocracy, the final formidable precapitalist force to be pushed out of the road, had been smashed and expropriated by the Civil War and Reconstruction.

The capitalist rulers of the industrial system were then like the Count of Monte Cristo when he burst from prison and exclaimed, with so much wealth and newly gained liberty at his command, "The world is mine!" And they have been acting on that premise ever since.

~

I would like now to make several observations on the economic and political development of American society from 1492 to the triumph of the capitalist class.

As has already been pointed out, private property in the means of production was nonexistent on this continent until the fifteenth century. Thereafter, as the settlers spread, the dominant trend was for all the means of production to pass into private hands and be exploited along such lines. The land, for example, which had been tribally held, was cut up and appropriated by individuals or corporations from one end of the country to the other.

After the victory of the Northern bankers, merchants, and manufacturers in the middle of the nineteenth century, this process moved on to a still higher plane. The means of production under private ownership became more and more concentrated in corporate hands. Today an individual might be able to build a single auto or airplane, but without many, many millions of dollars he would not be able to compete in the market with General Motors or Ford or Lockheed or Douglas. Even so big a magnate as Henry J. Kaiser found that out in auto.

Today there is hardly an acre of land without its title deed. In fact, the Civil War promoted this process through the Homestead Act, which gave 160 acres to private individuals, and through other acts of Congress that handed millions of acres over to railroad corporations. Insofar as the land was distributed to small farmers, this was progressive because it was the only way to hasten the development of agriculture under the given conditions.

It is impossible to detail here the settlement and building of the Midwest and the West, but certain consequences of capitalist expansion deserve mention. First, as a result of this capitalist expansion, the minds of average Americans, unlike those of the Indians, have been so molded by the institutions of private property that its standards can be thrown off only with difficulty. The Europeans penetrated the America of the Indians; and their descendants are venturing into outer space.

One extreme, absurd, but for that very reason most instructive, illustration of the effects of capitalist expansion on American consciousness appeared in a press dispatch from Illinois with the headline: "Who Is the Owner of Outer-Space; Chicagoan Insists that He Is." This news item followed:

> With plans for launching man-made earth satellites now in motion, the question was inevitable [inevitable, that is, to Americans believing in the sacredness of private ownership]: Who owns outer space?
>
> Most experts agreed that the question was over their heads. The rocket scientists said it was a problem for the international law experts. The lawyers said they had no precedents to go by. Only James T. Mangan, a fast-thinking Chicago press agent, has a firm answer to the question of space sovereignty. Mangan declares he owns outer space.
>
> To back up his claim, he has a deed filed with the Cook County (Chicago) Recorder. The deed, accepted after the state's attorney's office solemnly upheld the claim in a four-page legal opinion, seized "all space in all directions from the earth at midnight," December 20, 1948.
>
> Mangan declared that the statute of limitations for challenging the deed expires December 20, 1955, and added: "The government has no legal right to space without my permission."

The vanguard place of workers who are Black

Don't start with Blacks as an oppressed nationality. Start with the historical record of the vanguard place and weight of workers who are Black—a place and weight disproportionate to their percentage among the toilers in this country—in broad, proletarian-led social and political struggles in the United States.

This goes back to the closing years of the US Civil War and especially to the postwar battle for a radical reconstruction, in which Black toilers provided leadership in substantial parts of the South both to freed slaves and to exploited farmers and workers who were white.

It continued in the late nineteenth and early twentieth centuries in the labor battles that built the United Mine Workers—at a time when most unions were not only organized along craft lines but either excluded Blacks or segregated them in separate locals.

Sharecroppers, tenant farmers, and other rural toilers, both Black and white, waged struggles in the 1920s and through the Great Depression. Workers who were Black were in the front ranks of key battles that built the CIO industrial unions in the 1930s.

They were in the vanguard of working people during World War II who refused to subordinate or postpone struggles for justice in the name of "the patriotic war effort"—fighting discrimination in the war industries, protesting Jim Crow conditions in the armed forces, and demanding (unsuccessfully) that the Roosevelt administration and Democratic-dominated Congress pass federal legislation outlawing racist lynchings.

They were in the forefront of those who opposed that imperialist war. And many of us know firsthand the lasting social and political impact on the working class and labor movement today of the mass civil rights movement and rise of the Black liberation struggle from the mid-1950s through the early 1970s.

We're not speculating about the future. We're pointing to a historical record. It's a matter of fact. It's a mind-boggling record, it seems to me. It bowls you over.

The same cannot be said of the big majority of oppressed nations or nationalities in general in other parts of the world. But this *is* the political record of the largely proletarian Black nationality in the United States.

This *is* its specific political character since the defeat of chattel slavery, the effort to extend the victory in the Civil War throughout the South, and the beginning of the expansion of a modern hereditary proletariat in the US.

It is this dynamic that Trotsky, more than seven decades ago, was pointing to when he said it is possible "that the Negroes will become the most advanced section" of the working class, and "will proceed through self-determination to the proletarian dictatorship in a couple of gigantic strides, ahead of the great bloc of white workers." It was for that reason that he was "absolutely sure that they will in any case fight better than the white workers" on the whole.

JACK BARNES, 2009
Malcolm X, Black Liberation, and the Road to Workers Power

If this be madness, yet there is method in it. That method is the mainspring of the capitalist way of life. This gentleman, Mangan, is only logically extending to the exploration of outer space the same acquisitive creed which guided our founding fathers in taking over the American continent. This particular fanatic of private property thinks the same law is going to apply no matter how far into space we fly and no matter how far we go into the future. He differs from other exponents of capitalism only in the boldness and consistency of his private-property logic.

The second point I want to deal with is the interconnection between evolution and revolution. These two phases of social development are often opposed to each other as unconnected opposites, irreconcilable alternatives. What does American history teach us about them? The American people have already passed through two revolutionary periods in their national history, each the culmination of lengthy periods of social progress on the basis of previous achievements.

During the interval between revolutions, relatively small changes gradually occurred in people's lives. They consequently took the given framework of their lives for granted, viewed it as fixed and final, and found it hard to imagine a different way. The idea of revolutionary change in their own lives and lifetimes seemed fantastic or at least irrelevant. Yet it was during those very periods of evolutionary progress that often unnoticed accumulations of changes prepared more drastic change.

The new class interests, which grew powerful but remained unsatisfied, the social and political conflicts, which recurred but remained unresolved, the shifts in the relations of antagonistic social forces kept asserting themselves in a series of disturbances until they reached an acute stage. The people of this country were not reckless. They made every attempt to find reasonable compromises between the contending forces, and often arrived at them. But after a while, these truces turned out to be ineffectual and short-lived. The irrepressible conflict of social forces broke out at higher stages until the breaking point was reached.

Between the two revolutions in the US, small changes gradually occurred in people's lives. Revolutionary change seemed fantastic to most. Yet it was the unnoticed accumulations of change that prepared more drastic upheaval.

Look at the American colonists of 1763. They had just emerged—side-by-side with mother England—from a successful war against the French and allied Indian tribes. They did not anticipate that within ten years they would be fighting for their own freedom against England and alongside the very French monarchy they had fought in 1763. That would have been considered fantastic. Yet it happened only a little more than a decade later. Dr. Benjamin Rush, one of Pennsylvania's signers of the Declaration of Independence, observed in his *Autobiography* that:

> Not one man in a thousand contemplated or wished for the independence of our country in 1774, and but few of those who assented to it, foresaw the immense influence it would soon have upon the national and individual characters of the Americans.

So, too, the majority of Northerners, who enjoyed the economic boom in America from 1851 to 1857—the biggest boom in the nineteenth century preceding the Civil War—little reckoned that as the result of domestic processes accelerated by that very prosperity, the country was going to be split on the slave question four years after the depression of 1857. Instead, they reasoned: Hadn't there been a compromise with the slaveholders in 1850—and couldn't others be arrived at? Indeed, there were attempts at compromise up to the very outbreak of the Civil War, and even afterwards.

Of course, the Abolitionists at one extreme and the Southern "Fire-Eaters" at the other prophesied a different course of development and, in their own ways, prepared for the coming revolution. But these radical voices on the left and the right were few and far between.

These crucial episodes in American history demonstrate that, under conditions of class society, periods of gradual social *evolution* prepare forces for the *revolutionary* solution of the accumulated and unfinished problems of peoples and nations. This revolutionary cleanup in turn creates the premises for a new and higher stage of evolutionary progress. This alternation is demonstrated with exceptional clarity by American history in the eighteenth and nineteenth centuries.

It is important to note, as a third point in dealing with the consequences of capitalist development in the United States, that our national revolutions stemmed directly from native conditions. Neither was imported by "outside agitators," although some, like the English-born revolutionary leader Tom Paine, played important roles. The two revolutions came from the ripening of conflicts between internal social forces. But this is only one side of the matter. The domestic struggles in turn were connected with, conditioned, and determined by world economic and social development.

We pointed out earlier that the impetus for the overseas migration that changed the face of America came from the antifeudal bourgeois revolutions, which were transforming Europe; the conquest of our continent was an offshoot of those revolutions. The First American Revolution occurred during the era of commercial capitalism, which was the first stage in world capitalist development. Historically, it forms part of the series of bourgeois-democratic revolutions by which the capitalist class came to power on an international scale. The First American Revolution must be considered a child of the English bourgeois revolution of the mid-seventeenth century and a parent of sorts to the French bourgeois-democratic revolution of the late eighteenth century.

Trade in this era, not simply American but world trade, produced a powerful merchant class in the North, which was backed up by maritime workers and artisans in the coastal cities and by free farmers in the countryside. These became the shock troops of the Sons of Liberty. It is no accident that the bustling seaport of Boston, populated by rich merchants who wanted to get out from under the thumb of Great Britain and by robust waterfront workers, longshoremen, and sailors, stood in the forefront of the fight against Great Britain. Nor is it an accident that the revolutionary war itself was detonated by the British efforts to gag and strangle Boston.

The Second American Revolution took place at the time of the greatest expansion of industrial capitalism on both sides of the Atlantic. The years from 1848 to 1871 were punctuated by wars and revolutions. These conflicts did not mark the disintegration of world capital, as they have in the twentieth century, but finally gave the capitalist class unmitigated supremacy in America and a series of countries in Europe.

Crushing of Radical Reconstruction: worst defeat for US working class

By 1877, Radical Reconstruction had gone down to bloody defeat and not only Afro-Americans but the entire working class had suffered what remains the worst setback in its history.

The defeat was engineered by the dominant sectors of industrial and rising banking capital, a class that was incapable of carrying through a radical land reform in the old Confederacy and rightly feared the rise of a united working class in which Black and white artisans and industrial workers would come together as a powerful oppositional force, allied with free working farmers.

The rural poor and working class were forcibly divided along color lines in the years following 1877. The value of labor power was driven down and class solidarity crippled. Jim Crow, the system of extensive segregation, was legalized. Racism spread at an accelerated pace throughout the entire United States.

FARRELL DOBBS, 1980
Revolutionary Continuity:
Marxist Leadership in the United States
The Early Years, 1848–1917

The second stage of the bourgeois-democratic revolution in the United States, the Civil War, placed the Northern industrialists in the saddle. It was the outstanding revolutionary event of the entire period that began with the abortive French and German revolutions of 1848 and ended with the Franco-Prussian War and the Paris Commune of 1871. The decisive event of that period in world history was the US capitalists' victory in this country, which heralded their ascent to world power.

∾

With these lessons in mind, let us now look at the march of American society from the close of the Civil War period until today.

Having reaped the fruits of two successful revolutions, the capitalists began to enjoy them. For them, revolution in America was a thing of the past; the United States would advance by small slow steps. Indeed, there has been a significant evolution of capitalist society on the foundation of the achievements of its previous revolutions.

But in the dialectic of our national development, it is the very extraordinary expansion of the capitalist forces of production that has been preparing the elements for another showdown between class forces that belong to different stages of economic and social evolution.

Since 1878, there have been two major trends in operation in this country. The predominant one to date has been the growing concentration of economic, political, and cultural power in the hands of the monopolists. They have occasionally been challenged but never dislodged. Today they are open and insolent in the exercise of power. As Mr. Charles Wilson, head of both the biggest monopoly and the Defense Department, has said: "What's good for General Motors is good for the USA."

This echoes the assertion by an earlier absolute monarch, Louis XIV: "I am the state." The old regime of France had its funeral in 1789. Everything in this world—and this is especially true of political regimes and social systems under class society—includes within itself its own opposition, its own fatal opposition. This is certainly true of the power of capitalism, which breeds its own nemesis in the productive—and political—capacities of wage labor.

The irony is that the greater the wealth of the capitalist class, the stronger becomes the social position of the exploited workers from whom this wealth is derived. Ever since capitalists and wage workers together came into existence, there have been differences, friction, outbursts of conflict, strikes, lockouts, between these two classes and sections of them. They arise from the very nature of their relations, which are antagonistic.

By and large, up to now, these conflicts have never gone beyond the bounds of the basic political and economic structure laid down by the Civil War. They have been subdued, reconciled, or smoothed over. Despite all disturbances, the monopolist rulers have entrenched themselves more firmly in their paramount positions.

However, a closer scrutiny of the development discloses that the working class occupies an increasingly influential, though still subordinate, place in our national life.

The question presents itself with renewed force: Will this situation of class stalemate—with the workers in a secondary position—continue indefinitely? The capitalists naturally answer that it can and must be so. Furthermore, they do everything from teaching in school the perpetual existence of the established class structure to passing anti-labor laws to insure the continuance of the status quo. The union officialdom, for their part, go along with this general proposition.

Neither the capitalist spokesmen nor the AFL-CIO officialdom will find any precedent in American history to reinforce their expectations of an indefinite maintenance of the status quo. That is one lesson from our national past that the "long view" of socialism emphasizes. For many

Organized labor has within its grasp enough political strength, not to speak of economic and social capacities, to be the sovereign force in this country.

TESSA WORLEY/TOWNSQUARE MEDIA

Above: In the 1930s Minneapolis Teamsters waged strike battles that made the city a union stronghold and organized 250,000 trucking workers into the union across 11 states. Shown here is the volunteer Union Defense Guard formed in Minneapolis, which successfully blocked organizing drives by fascist Silver Shirts.

Below: Some 1,100 members of United Mine Workers union in Alabama walked off the job in April 2021 against Warrior Met Coal. Miners demanded bosses reverse concessions forced on them in 2016, including wage cuts, forced overtime at lower premium pay, increased health-care costs, and slashing of paid holidays.

years, despite occasional tiffs, the American colonists got along with their mother country and even cherished the tie. Then came a very rapid and radical reversal in relations, a duel to the end.

The same held true of the long coexistence of the Northern free states and Southern slavery. For sixty years, the Northerners had to play second fiddle to the Southern slave autocracy until the majority of people in the country came to believe that this situation would endure indefinitely. The slave owners, like the capitalists of today, taught that their "American way of life" was the crown jewel of civilization.

But once the new combination of progressive forces was obliged to assert itself, the maturing differences broke out in a civil war which disposed of the old order. The political collaborators of yesterday turned into irreconcilable foes on the morrow.

Just as the British tyrants and the Southern slaveholders, each in their day, mustered all their resources to hold back the oncoming revolutionary forces in this land, so do the agents of the American plutocracy today. Will the monopolists succeed where their forerunners failed? Let us consider this question.

The high point of a revolutionary process consists in the transfer of supreme power from one class to another. What are the prevailing relationships of power in the United States? All basic decisions on foreign and domestic policy are made by the top capitalist circles to advance their aims and interests. Labor may be able to modify this or that decision or policy, but its influence does no more than curb the political power exercised by the monopolists.

However, there is a remarkable anomaly in such a relationship of forces. The now united union movement, the

AFL-CIO—which in 1955 brought the American Federation of Labor and the Congress of Industrial Organizations together—has millions of members. With their families, followers, and friends, organized labor has within its own grasp enough political strength, not to speak of its economic and social capacities, to be the sovereign force in this country.

Motion toward the formation of an independent party of labor based on the trade unions could only be the product of a fighting labor movement in the process of transforming itself. It would have highly revolutionizing implications, regardless of the intentions or announced program of its organizers.

Any such move on a massive scale would portend a shift in the power of supreme decision in the United States, just as the coming to Washington of the Republican Party in 1860 signified the shift of power away from the slaveholders to the Northern industrialists.

The Republican leaders of 1861 did not have revolutionary intentions. They headed a reformist party. They wanted to restrict the power of the slaveholders. But to do this involved upsetting the established balance of class forces. The slaveholders recognized the threat to their supremacy far more clearly and felt it more keenly than did the Northern Republican leaders themselves. That is why they initiated a counterrevolutionary assault in order to retrieve the power they had previously possessed.

The parallel with any national assumption of political predominance by the labor movement, even in a reformist way, is plain to see. Is such a shift possible?

A succession of crucial shifts of power has marked the onward movement of the American people: from Britain to the colonial merchants and planters in the eighteenth century; and from the Southern slavocracy to the industrial capitalists in the nineteenth century. The thrust in the present period of our national history is toward another such colossal shift, this time from the ruling plutocracy to the rising working class and its allies among the working farmers and oppressed minorities.

The whole course of economic, social, and political development in this country and in this century points to such a shift in power. Of course, the working class is far from predominant yet, and even less conscious of its historical mission. But, from the standpoint of the long view, it is most important to note the different rates of growth in the economic, social, and political potentialities of the respective contenders for supreme power.

Reviewing this country's history from 1876 on, together with the rate of growth of the working class on a world scale, the balance of forces has been shifting, despite all oscillations, toward the side of working people. Nothing whatsoever, including imperialist war, federal antilabor laws, or the Cold War witch-hunt, has been able to stop the momentum.

The supreme merit of scientific socialism is that it enables us to participate in this process by understanding it, by striving to influence it through all its stages, by giving it proper direction and speeding it up so that its great aims can be achieved most economically and efficiently. This job can be done in an organized fashion only through a revolutionary leadership and a Marxist party that understands its indispensable educational and organizational functions in the process.

∼

It was a decisive step in the process of evolution, we pointed out, when the first creature acquired a backbone. There have been many relapses in the movement of history, especially in the world-shaking struggles of our own generation. Many people became frightened by the immensity of the tasks or crushed by adversity to the point of losing their moral and intellectual backbones and of losing sight of the direction of social evolution.

The supreme lesson of both world history and American history, however, is that the forces making for the advancement of mankind have overcome the most formidable obstacles and have won out in the end. Otherwise, we should not be here to tell the tale or to help in making its next chapter.

The American people will bring forward in the future, as they have at critical times in the past, more audacious men and women with a vision of a new world in the making. These fighting leaders and leading fighters, guided by "the long view" of Marxism, will prove in practice that the socialist prospects of humanity, including the American people, are not so distant as they now appear.

The epoch of the bourgeoisie and the forging of its gravediggers

Karl Marx and Frederick Engels

The history of all hitherto existing society* is the history of class struggles.

Freeman and slave, patrician and plebeian, lord and serf,

---

* That is, all *written* history. In 1847, the prehistory of society, the social organization existing previous to recorded history, was all but unknown. Since then, Haxthausen discovered common ownership of land in Russia, Maurer proved it to be the social foundation from which all Teutonic races started in history, and by and by village communities were found to be, or to have been, the primitive form of society everywhere from India to Ireland. The inner organization of this primitive communistic society was laid bare, in its typical form, by Morgan's crowning discovery of the true nature of the *gens* and its relation to the *tribe*.

With the dissolution of these primeval communities, society begins to be differentiated into separate and finally antagonistic classes. I have attempted to retrace this process of dissolution in *The Origin of the Family, Private Property and the State.*—NOTE BY ENGELS TO 1888 ENGLISH EDITION

From the opening pages of the Communist Manifesto, founding program of the revolutionary workers movement. It was first published in February 1848.

guildmaster* and journeyman, in a word, oppressor and oppressed, stood in constant opposition to one another, carried on an uninterrupted, now hidden, now open fight, a fight that each time ended either in a revolutionary re-constitution of society at large or in the common ruin of the contending classes.

The history of all hitherto existing society is the history of class struggles.

In the earlier epochs of history, we find almost every-where a complicated arrangement of society into various orders, a manifold gradation of social rank. In ancient Rome we have patricians, knights, plebeians, slaves; in the Middle Ages, feudal lords, vassals, guildmasters, journey-men, apprentices, serfs; in almost all of these classes, again, subordinate gradations.

The modern bourgeois society† that has sprouted from the ruins of feudal society has not done away with class antagonisms. It has but established new classes, new con-ditions of oppression, new forms of struggle in place of the old ones.

Our epoch, the epoch of the bourgeoisie, possesses, how-ever, this distinctive feature: it has simplified the class an-tagonisms. Society as a whole is more and more splitting up

---

* Guildmaster, that is, a full member of a guild, a master within, not a head of a guild.—NOTE BY ENGELS TO 1888 ENGLISH EDITION

† By bourgeoisie is meant the class of modern capitalists, owners of the means of social production and employers of wage labor. By proletariat, the class of modern wage-laborers who, having no means of production of their own, are reduced to selling their labor power in order to live.— NOTE BY ENGELS TO 1888 ENGLISH EDITION

into two great hostile camps, into two great classes directly facing each other: bourgeoisie and proletariat.

From the serfs of the Middle Ages sprang the chartered burghers of the earliest towns. From these burgesses the first elements of the bourgeoisie were developed.

The discovery of America, the rounding of the Cape of Good Hope, opened up fresh ground for the rising bourgeoisie. The East Indian and Chinese markets, the colonization of America, trade with the colonies, the increase in the means of exchange and in commodities generally, gave to commerce, to navigation, to industry, an impulse never before known, and thereby, to the revolutionary element in the tottering feudal society, a rapid development.

The feudal system of industry, under which industrial production was monopolized by closed guilds, now no longer sufficed for the growing wants of the new markets. The manufacturing system took its place. The guildmasters were pushed to one side by the manufacturing middle class; division of labor between the different corporate guilds vanished in the face of division of labor in each single workshop.

Meantime the markets kept ever growing, the demand ever rising. Even manufacture no longer sufficed. Thereupon, steam and machinery revolutionized industrial production. The place of manufacture was taken by the giant, modern industry, the place of the industrial middle class, by industrial millionaires, the leaders of whole industrial armies, the modern bourgeois.

Modern industry has established the world market, for which the discovery of America paved the way. This market has given an immense development to commerce, to navigation, to communication by land. This development has, in its turn, reacted on the extension of industry; and in proportion as industry, commerce, navigation, railways extended, in the same proportion the bourgeoisie developed, increased its capital, and pushed into the background every class handed down from the Middle Ages.

We see, therefore, how the modern bourgeoisie is itself the product of a long course of development, of a series of revolutions in the modes of production and of exchange.

Each step in the development of the bourgeoisie was accompanied by a corresponding political advance of that class. An oppressed class under the sway of the feudal nobility, an armed and self-governing association in the medieval commune;* here independent urban republic (as in Italy and Germany), there taxable "third estate" of the monarchy (as in France), afterwards, in the period of manufacture proper, serving either the semifeudal or the absolute monarchy as a counterpoise against the nobility, and, in fact, cornerstone of the great monarchies in general, the bourgeoisie has at last, since the establishment of modern industry and of the world market, conquered for itself, in the modern representative state, exclusive political sway. The executive of the modern state is but a committee for managing the common affairs of the whole bourgeoisie.

The bourgeoisie, historically, has played a most revolutionary part.

The bourgeoisie, wherever it has gotten the upper hand, has put an end to all feudal, patriarchal, idyllic relations.

---

* "Commune" was the name taken, in France, by the nascent towns even before they had conquered from their feudal lords and masters local self-government and political rights as the "Third Estate." Generally speaking, for the economic development of the bourgeoisie, England is here taken as the typical country; for its political development, France.—NOTE BY ENGELS TO 1888 ENGLISH EDITION

This was the name given their urban communities by the townsmen of Italy and France, after they had purchased or wrested their initial rights of self-government from their feudal lords.—NOTE BY ENGELS TO 1890 GERMAN EDITION

It has pitilessly torn asunder the motley feudal ties that bound man to his "natural superiors," and has left remaining no other nexus between man and man than naked self-interest, than callous "cash payment." It has drowned the most heavenly ecstasies of religious fervor, of chivalrous enthusiasm, of philistine sentimentalism, in the icy water of egotistical calculation. It has resolved personal worth into exchange value, and in place of the numberless indefeasible chartered freedoms, has set up that single, unconscionable freedom—free trade. In one word, for exploitation, veiled by religious and political illusions, it has substituted naked, shameless, direct, brutal exploitation.

The bourgeoisie cannot exist without constantly revolutionizing the instruments and relations of production, and the whole relations of society.

The bourgeoisie has stripped of its halo every occupation hitherto honored and looked up to with reverent awe. It has converted the physician, the lawyer, the priest, the poet, the man of science, into its paid wage-laborers.

The bourgeoisie has torn away from the family its sentimental veil and has reduced the family relation to a mere money relation.

The bourgeoisie has disclosed how it came to pass that the brutal display of vigor in the Middle Ages, which reactionists so much admire, found its fitting complement in the most slothful indolence. It has been the first to show what man's activity can bring about. It has accomplished

wonders far surpassing Egyptian pyramids, Roman aque-
ducts, and Gothic cathedrals; it has conducted expeditions
that put in the shade all former exoduses of nations and
crusades.

The bourgeoisie cannot exist without constantly revolutionizing the instruments of production, and thereby the
relations of production, and with them the whole relations
of society. Conservation of the old modes of production in
unaltered form was, on the contrary, the first condition of
existence for all earlier industrial classes. Constant revolutionizing of production, uninterrupted disturbance of
all social conditions, everlasting uncertainty and agitation
distinguish the bourgeois epoch from all earlier ones. All
fixed, fast-frozen relations, with their train of ancient and
venerable prejudices and opinions, are swept away, all new-
formed ones become antiquated before they can ossify. All
that is solid melts into air, all that is holy is profaned, and
man is at last compelled to face, with sober senses, his real
conditions of life and his relations with his kind.

The need of a constantly expanding market for its products chases the bourgeoisie over the whole surface of the
globe. It must nestle everywhere, settle everywhere, establish connections everywhere.

The bourgeoisie has, through its exploitation of the
world market, given a cosmopolitan character to production and consumption in every country. To the great
chagrin of reactionists, it has drawn from under the feet
of industry the national ground on which it stood. All
old-established national industries have been destroyed
or are daily being destroyed. They are dislodged by new
industries, whose introduction becomes a life-and-death
question for all civilized nations, by industries that no
longer work up indigenous raw material, but raw material drawn from the remotest zones; industries whose

Europe's discovery of America opened fresh ground for the rising bourgeoisie. It gave to commerce, to navigation, to industry, an impulse never before known, and thereby, to the revolutionary element in the tottering feudal society, a rapid development.

Colón, Panama, 1855. Six decades before the Panama Canal, the Panama Railroad was completed, crossing the isthmus. It carried passengers and goods headed to California, which was booming in wake of the Gold Rush.

This link between the Atlantic and Pacific Oceans, much shorter than the sea route around South America, revolutionized world capitalist trade.

products are consumed not only at home, but in every quarter of the globe.

In place of the old wants, satisfied by the productions of the country, we find new wants, requiring for their satisfaction the products of distant lands and climes. In place of the old local and national seclusion and self-sufficiency, we have intercourse in every direction, universal interdependence of nations. And as in material, so also in intellectual production. The intellectual creations of individual nations become common property. National one-sidedness and narrow-mindedness become more and more impossible, and from the numerous national and local literatures, there arises a world literature.

> **What earlier century had even a presentiment that such productive forces slumbered in the lap of social labor?**

The bourgeoisie, by the rapid improvement of all instruments of production, by the immensely facilitated means of communication, draws all, even the most barbarian, nations into civilization. The cheap prices of its commodities are the heavy artillery with which it batters down all Chinese walls, with which it forces the barbarians' intensely obstinate hatred of foreigners to capitulate. It compels all nations, on pain of extinction, to adopt the bourgeois mode of production; it compels them to introduce what it calls civilization into their midst, i.e., to become bourgeois themselves. In one word, it creates a world after its own image.

The bourgeoisie has subjected the country to the rule of the towns. It has created enormous cities, has greatly increased the urban population as compared with the rural, and has thus rescued a considerable part of the population from the idiocy of rural life. Just as it has made the country dependent on the towns, so it has made barbarian and semibarbarian countries dependent on the civilized ones, nations of peasants on nations of bourgeois, the East on the West.

The bourgeoisie keeps more and more doing away with the scattered state of the population, of the means of production, and of property. It has agglomerated population, centralized means of production, and has concentrated property in a few hands. The necessary consequence of this was political centralization. Independent, or but loosely connected provinces, with separate interests, laws, governments, and systems of taxation, became lumped together into one nation, with one government, one code of laws, one national class interest, one frontier, and one customs tariff.

The bourgeoisie, during its rule of scarce one hundred years, has created more massive and more colossal productive forces than have all preceding generations together. Subjection of nature's forces to man, machinery, application of chemistry to industry and agriculture, steam navigation, railways, electric telegraphs, clearing of whole continents for cultivation, canalization of rivers, whole populations conjured out of the ground—what earlier century had even a presentiment that such productive forces slumbered in the lap of social labor?

We see then: the means of production and of exchange, on whose foundation the bourgeoisie built itself up, were generated in feudal society. At a certain stage in the development of these means of production and of exchange, the

conditions under which feudal society produced and exchanged, the feudal organization of agriculture and manufacturing industry, in one word, the feudal relations of
property, became no longer compatible with the already
developed productive forces; they became so many fetters.
They had to be burst asunder; they were burst asunder.

Into their place stepped free competition, accompanied
by a social and political constitution adapted to it and by
the economic and political sway of the bourgeois class.

A similar movement is going on before our own eyes.
Modern bourgeois society with its relations of production,
of exchange, and of property, a society that has conjured
up such gigantic means of production and of exchange, is
like the sorcerer who is no longer able to control the powers of the nether world whom he has called up by his spells.
For many a decade past, the history of industry and commerce is but the history of the revolt of modern productive
forces against modern conditions of production, against
the property relations that are the conditions for the existence of the bourgeoisie and of its rule.

It is enough to mention the commercial crises that by
their periodic return put on trial, each time more threat-
eningly, the existence of the entire bourgeois society. In
these crises a great part not only of the existing products,
but also of the previously created productive forces are
periodically destroyed. In these crises there breaks out an
epidemic that, in all earlier epochs, would have seemed an
absurdity—the epidemic of over-production. Society suddenly finds itself put back into a state of momentary barbarism; it appears as if a famine, a universal war of devasta-
tion, had cut off the supply of every means of subsistence;
industry and commerce seem to be destroyed.

And why? Because there is too much civilization, too
much means of subsistence, too much industry, too much

commerce. The productive forces at the disposal of society no longer tend to further the development of the conditions of bourgeois property; on the contrary, they have become too powerful for these conditions, by which they are fettered, and so soon as they overcome these fetters, they bring disorder into the whole of bourgeois society, endanger the existence of bourgeois property. The conditions of bourgeois society are too narrow to comprise the wealth created by them.

And how does the bourgeoisie get over these crises? On the one hand by enforced destruction of a mass of productive forces; on the other, by the conquest of new markets and by the more thorough exploitation of the old ones. That is to say, by paving the way for more extensive and more destructive crises and by diminishing the means whereby crises are prevented.

The weapons with which the bourgeoisie felled feudalism to the ground are now turned against the bourgeoisie itself.

But not only has the bourgeoisie forged the weapons that bring death to itself; it has also called into existence the men who are to wield those weapons—the modern working class—the proletarians.

In proportion as the bourgeoisie, i.e., capital, is developed, in the same proportion is the proletariat, the modern working class, developed—a class of laborers, who live only so long as they find work and who find work only so long as their labor increases capital. These laborers, who must sell themselves piecemeal, are a commodity, like every other article of commerce, and are consequently exposed to all the vicissitudes of competition, to all the fluctuations of the market.

Owing to the extensive use of machinery, and to division of labor, the work of the proletarians has lost all individual character and, consequently, all charm for the workman. He becomes an appendage of the machine, and it is only the most simple, most monotonous, and most easily acquired knack that is required of him. Hence, the cost of production of a workman is restricted, almost entirely, to the means of subsistence that he requires for his maintenance and for the propagation of his race.

But the price of a commodity, and therefore also of labor power, is equal to its cost of production. In proportion, therefore, as the repulsiveness of the work increases, the wage decreases. Nay more, in proportion as the use of machinery and division of labor increases, in the same proportion the burden of toil also increases, whether by prolongation of the working hours, by increase of the work exacted in a given time, or by increased speed of machinery, etc.

Modern industry has converted the little workshop of the patriarchal master into the great factory of the industrial capitalist. Masses of laborers, crowded into the factory, are organized like soldiers. As privates of the industrial army they are placed under the command of a perfect hierarchy of officers and sergeants. Not only are they slaves of the bourgeois class and of the bourgeois state; they are daily and hourly enslaved by the machine, by the overlooker, and, above all, by the individual bourgeois manufacturer himself. The more openly this despotism proclaims gain to be its end and aim, the more petty, the more hateful, and the more embittering it is.

The less the skill and exertion of strength implied in manual labor, in other words, the more modern industry becomes developed, the more is the labor power of men superseded by that of women. Differences of age and sex have no longer any distinctive social validity for the working class. All are instruments of labor, more or less expensive to use, according to their age and sex.

No sooner is the exploitation of the laborer by the manufacturer, so far, at an end, and he receives his wages in cash, than he is set upon by the other portions of the bourgeoisie, the landlord, the shopkeeper, the pawnbroker, etc.

As use of machinery and division of labor increases, so does the burden of toil—through longer working hours, increased work in a given time, or greater machine speed.

The lower strata of the middle class—the small trades people, shopkeepers, and retired tradesmen generally, the handicraftsmen and peasants—all these sink gradually into the proletariat, partly because their diminutive capital does not suffice for the scale on which modern industry is carried on and is swamped in the competition with the large capitalists, partly because their specialized skill is rendered worthless by new methods of production. Thus the proletariat is recruited from all classes of the population.

The proletariat goes through various stages of development. With its birth begins its struggle with the bourgeoisie. At first the contest is carried on by individual laborers, then by the workers of a factory, then by the operatives of one trade, in one locality, against the individual bourgeois who directly exploits them. They direct their attacks not against the bourgeois conditions of production, but against the instruments of production themselves; they destroy imported wares that compete with their labor, they smash to pieces machinery, they set factories ablaze, they seek to restore by force the vanished status of the work-man of the Middle Ages.

At this stage the laborers still form an incoherent mass scattered over the whole country and broken up by their mutual competition. If anywhere they unite to form more compact bodies, this is not yet the consequence of their own active union but of the union of the bourgeoisie, which class, in order to attain its own political ends, is compelled to set the whole proletariat in motion and is moreover yet, for a time, able to do so. At this stage, there-fore, the proletarians do not fight their enemies, but the enemies of their enemies, the remnants of absolute mon-archy, the landowners, the nonindustrial bourgeois, the petty bourgeoisie. Thus the whole historical movement is concentrated in the hands of the bourgeoisie; every vic-tory so obtained is a victory for the bourgeoisie.

But with the development of industry the proletariat not only increases in number; it becomes concentrated in greater masses, its strength grows, and it feels that strength more. The various interests and conditions of life within the ranks of the proletariat are more and more equalized, in proportion as machinery obliterates all distinctions of labor and nearly everywhere reduces wages to the same low level. The growing competition among the bourgeois, and the resulting commercial crises, make the wages of the workers ever more fluctuating. The unceasing improve-ment of machinery, ever more rapidly developing, makes their livelihood more and more precarious; the collisions between individual workmen and individual bourgeois take more and more the character of collisions between two classes. Thereupon the workers begin to form com-binations (trades unions) against the bourgeois; they club together in order to keep up the rate of wages; they found permanent associations in order to make provision before-

Workers form combinations (trade unions) to keep up wages. Now and then they are victorious, but only for a time. The real fruit of their battles lies in the ever-expanding union of the workers.

IBEW LOCAL 304

Workers at Frito-Lay pushed back brutal schedules they called "suicide shifts" during July 2021 strike in Topeka, Kansas. Gains won by 600 members of Bakery, Confectionary, Tobacco Workers, and Grain Millers encouraged other workers to use their unions to fight employer attacks on wages, benefits, and job conditions.

hand for these occasional revolts. Here and there the contest breaks out into riots.

Now and then the workers are victorious, but only for
a time. The real fruit of their battles lies, not in the immediate result, but in the ever-expanding union of the
workers. This union is helped on by the improved means
of communication that are created by modern industry
and that place the workers of different localities in contact
with one another. It was just this contact that was needed
to centralize the numerous local struggles, all of the same
character, into one national struggle between classes. But
every class struggle is a political struggle. And that union,
to attain which the burghers of the Middle Ages, with their
miserable highways, required centuries, the modern proletarians, thanks to railways, achieve in a few years.

This organization of the proletarians into a class, and
consequently into a political party, is continually being
upset again by the competition between the workers themselves. But it ever rises up again, stronger, firmer, mightier.
It compels legislative recognition of particular interests of
the workers, by taking advantage of the divisions among
the bourgeoisie itself. Thus the ten-hours bill in England
was carried.

Altogether collisions between the classes of the old society further, in many ways, the course of development of
the proletariat. The bourgeoisie finds itself involved in a
constant battle. At first with the aristocracy; later on, with
those portions of the bourgeoisie itself whose interests
have become antagonistic to the progress of industry; at
all times, with the bourgeoisie of foreign countries. In all
these battles it sees itself compelled to appeal to the proletariat, to ask for its help, and thus to drag it into the political arena. The bourgeoisie itself, therefore, supplies the
proletariat with its own elements of political and general

education; in other words, it furnishes the proletariat with weapons for fighting the bourgeoisie.

Further, as we have already seen, entire sections of the ruling classes are, by the advance of industry, precipitated into the proletariat or are at least threatened in their conditions of existence. These also supply the proletariat with fresh elements of enlightenment and progress.

> **Of all the classes that stand face to face with the bourgeoisie today, the proletariat alone is a really revolutionary class.**

Finally, in times when the class struggle nears the decisive hour, the process of dissolution going on within the ruling class, in fact within the whole range of old society, assumes such a violent, glaring character, that a small section of the ruling class cuts itself adrift, and joins the revolutionary class, the class that holds the future in its hands. Just as, therefore, at an earlier period a section of the nobility went over to the bourgeoisie, so now a portion of the bourgeoisie goes over to the proletariat, and in particular, a portion of the bourgeois ideologists who have raised themselves to the level of comprehending theoretically the historical movement as a whole.

Of all the classes that stand face to face with the bourgeoisie today, the proletariat alone is a really revolutionary class. The other classes decay and finally disappear in the face of modern industry; the proletariat is its special and essential product.

The lower middle class, the small manufacturer, the shop-keeper, the artisan, the peasant, all these fight against the bourgeoisie to save from extinction their existence as fractions of the middle class. They are therefore not revolutionary, but conservative. Nay more, they are reactionary, for they try to roll back the wheel of history. If by chance they are revolutionary, they are so only in view of their impending transfer into the proletariat, they thus defend not their present, but their future interests, they desert their own standpoint to place themselves at that of the proletariat.

The proletarian movement is the self-conscious, independent movement of the immense majority, in the interests of the immense majority.

The "dangerous class," the social scum, that passively rotting mass thrown off by the lowest layers of the old society, may, here and there, be swept into the movement by a proletarian revolution; its conditions of life, however, prepare it far more for the part of a bribed tool of reactionary intrigue.

In the conditions of the proletariat, those of old society at large are already virtually swamped. The proletarian is without property; his relation to his wife and children has no longer anything in common with the bourgeois family relations; modern industrial labor, modern subjection to capital, the same in England as in France, in America as in Germany, has stripped him of every trace of national character. Law, morality, religion are to him so many bourgeois prejudices, behind which lurk in ambush just as many bourgeois interests.

All the preceding classes that got the upper hand sought to fortify their already acquired status by subjecting society at large to their conditions of appropriation. The proletarians cannot become masters of the productive forces of society except by abolishing their own previous mode of appropriation and thereby also every other previous mode of appropriation. They have nothing of their own to secure and to fortify; their mission is to destroy all previous securities for, and insurances of, individual property.

All previous historical movements were movements of minorities, or in the interest of minorities. The proletarian movement is the self-conscious, independent movement of the immense majority, in the interests of the immense majority. The proletariat, the lowest stratum of our present society, cannot stir, cannot raise itself up, without the whole superincumbent strata of official society being sprung into the air.

Though not in substance, yet in form, the struggle of the proletariat with the bourgeoisie is at first a national struggle. The proletariat of each country must, of course, first of all settle matters with its own bourgeoisie.

In depicting the most general phases of the development of the proletariat, we traced the more or less veiled civil war, raging within existing society, up to the point where that war breaks out into open revolution and where the violent overthrow of the bourgeoisie lays the foundation for the sway of the proletariat.

Hitherto, every form of society has been based, as we have already seen, on the antagonism of oppressing and oppressed classes. But in order to oppress a class, certain conditions must be assured to it under which it can, at least, continue its slavish existence. The serf, in the period of serfdom, raised himself to membership in the commune, just as the petty bourgeois, under the yoke of the feudal absolutism, managed to develop into a bourgeois. The modern laborer, on the contrary, instead of rising with the progress of industry, sinks deeper and deeper below the conditions of existence of his own class. He becomes a pauper, and pauperism develops more rapidly than population and wealth. And here it becomes evident that the bourgeoisie is unfit any longer to be the ruling class in society and to impose its conditions of existence upon society as an overriding law. It is unfit to rule because it is incompetent to assure an existence to its slave within his slavery, because it cannot help letting him sink into such a state that it has to feed him, instead of being fed by him. Society can no longer live under this bourgeoisie; in other words, its existence is no longer compatible with society.

The essential condition for the existence and for the sway of the bourgeois class is the formation and augmentation of capital; the condition for capital is wage labor. Wage labor rests exclusively on competition between the laborers. The advance of industry, whose involuntary promoter is the bourgeoisie, replaces the isolation of the laborers, due to competition, by their revolutionary combination, due to association. The development of modern industry, therefore, cuts from under its feet the very foundation on which the bourgeoisie produces and appropriates products. What the bourgeoisie, therefore, produces, above all, is its own gravediggers. Its fall and the victory of the proletariat are equally inevitable.

~

In what relation do the communists stand to the proletarians as a whole?

The communists do not form a separate party opposed to other working-class parties.

They have no interests separate and apart from those of the proletariat as a whole.

They do not set up any sectarian principles of their own, by which to shape and mold the proletarian movement.

The theoretical conclusions of the communists merely express actual relations springing from an existing class struggle, from a historical movement going on under our very eyes.

The communists are distinguished from the other working-class parties by this only: (1) In the national struggles of the proletarians of the different countries, they point out and bring to the front the common interests of the entire proletariat, independently of all nationality. (2) In the various stages of development which the struggle of the working class against the bourgeoisie has to pass through, they always and everywhere represent the interests of the movement as a whole.

The communists, therefore, are on the one hand, practically, the most advanced and resolute section of the working-class parties of every country, that section which pushes forward all others; on the other hand, theoretically, they have over the great mass of the proletariat the advantage of clearly understanding the line of march, the conditions, and the ultimate general results of the proletarian movement.

The immediate aim of the communists is the same as that of all the other proletarian parties: formation of the

proletariat into a class, overthrow of the bourgeois supremacy, conquest of political power by the proletariat.

The theoretical conclusions of the communists are in no
way based on ideas or principles that have been invented,
or discovered, by this or that would-be universal reformer.

They merely express, in general terms, actual relations
springing from an existing class struggle, from a historical
movement going on under our very eyes.

INDEX

1619 Project, 30–31, 36–40

Abolitionists, 134
Acropolis (Athens), 88
AFL-CIO, 21, 138, 141
Africa, 22, 30, 107, 115, 119–20
Agassiz, Louis, 24–25
Agriculture, 55, 57, 91, 98, 100, 123,
   153–54
   improvements in, 85, 88, 92,
      96–97, 128
   Indigenous peoples'
      contributions to, 106–7, 112
   See also individual crops;
      Farmers, farming; Food
Alaska, 106
Alcohol, 63
Algeria, independence struggle, 13
Alphabet, 112
American Committee for the
   Defense of Leon Trotsky, 7–8
American Federation of Labor
   (AFL), 21, 141
American Museum of Natural
   History, 72
American Revolution, First (1775–81),
   119–23, 133
American Revolution, Second. *See*
   Civil War (US, 1861–65)
"American Way of Life," 117, 132, 140
Americas, European colonization
   of, 18, 63, 104, 106–15, 117, 147,
   151
   See also Indigenous peoples

Amphibians, 74–75, 77–79
Andes Mountains (Incas), 109
Animals, 17–18, 25, 46, 51, 59–60,
   87, 90–91, 94
   and climate, 55, 92
   communication by, 49–50
   despoliation of nature by, 52, 57
   domestication of, 53, 55–57,
      84–85, 88, 92, 109
   as humanity's ancestors, 17–18,
      25, 46, 48, 53, 55, 59–60, 69, 78,
      80–82, 84, 90, 105
   See also individual species
Anti-Dühring (Engels), 28–29
Apes, 43–53, 78–80
Appomattox, Virginia, 39
Arabs, 63
Army of Northern Virginia
   (Confederate), 38–39
Artisans, 87–89, 93, 100, 106–7, 119,
   135–36, 162
Asia, 60, 92, 98, 106–7, 109–10
Astraspis (early vertebrate), 73
Astronomy, 109
Athens, 88
Austen, Jane, 23
Aztecs (Mexico), 109, 114

Babylon, 96
Backboned animals (vertebrates),
   46, 72–78
Bakery, Confectionary, Tobacco
   Workers union (Frito-Lay
   strike), 159

Barbarism, 27–28, 90, 92–94, 100, 102,
    105, 109–10, 117–18, 127, 152–54
Barnes, Jack, 21, 39, 130–31
Belgium, 34
Bering Strait, 106, 108
Bible, account of creation in, 25, 74
Black struggle, US, 8, 21–22, 36–39,
    119, 127, 130–31, 136
Bolshevik Party, 8, 36, 103
Boston, 121, 135
Bourgeoisie, 10–11, 63, 65, 70, 85,
    104, 114, 117–20, 146–64
  concentration of wealth within,
    147–48, 150, 155
  political power won by, 148–49,
    152–54
    dictatorship of capital, 16
  proletarian struggle against,
    40–41, 130–31, 139, 155–58,
    160–61, 163–66
  See also Americas, European
    colonization of; Capitalism;
    Feudalism; Revolutions
Bow and arrow, 84, 87
Brain, 17, 50, 53, 55–56, 61, 78–80
Brandeis University, 23–24
Brazil, 47, 62
Bronze Age (approx. 3300 BC–1200
    BC), 87–88
Bulgaria, 83

California, 69, 90, 105, 118
"Cancel culture," 23–25
Cannibalism, 29, 53, 97–98
Capital (Marx), 6, 18, 31, 33–34
Capitalism, 10, 15–16, 18, 29, 36–37,
    39–40, 64–65, 71, 89, 97–101
  and precapitalist societies, 98,
    104, 116, 120, 128
  and feudalism, 94, 97–98, 102,
    110, 113, 117–18, 120, 135, 145–49,
    153–55, 157–58, 160, 163–64

Capitalism (*continued*)
  and chattel slavery, 36–37, 122–24,
    127, 131
  crises of, 71, 154–55, 158
  expansion of, 36, 63–65, 69, 100,
    113–23, 128–29, 147–48, 152–53
  and "human nature," 18
Capitalism, classes in conflict
  within, 36–37, 63, 76, 99–102,
    104–6, 113–15, 127–28, 156–58,
    160–66
  oppressed, 6, 64, 102, 104, 132–33,
    136–38, 140–47, 153–54, 156–64
  middle, 71, 147, 157–58, 161–62
  ruling, 36–37, 63–65, 123–25,
    127–28, 135, 138–40
    gravediggers, creates its own,
      103, 156, 160–61, 164
    racial divisions, promotion
      of, 40
  See also Working class
Capitalism, commercial, industrial,
  and monopoly
  commercial, 100, 113–14, 124,
    135–36
  industrial, 67, 100–101, 115, 122,
    126–27, 135–36, 141–42, 147,
    153, 156
  monopoly, 101, 137
Capitalist way of life. *See*
  "American Way of Life"
Caribbean, 22, 36, 108–9
Castro, Fidel, 36
Catlin, George, 116
Cattle, 55, 92, 109
Cave drawings, 83, 92
Censorship, 23–24
Children, 59–60, 70, 79, 91, 162
China, 21–22, 117, 147
Chinese Revolution (1926–27), 71
"Citizen of the world" (Leon
  Trotsky), 97–98

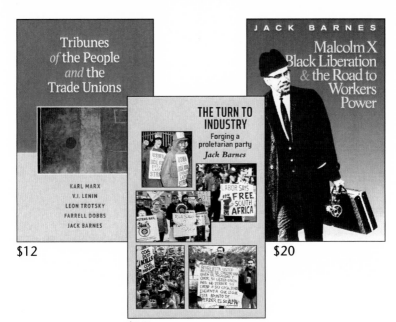

$12

$15

$20

Three books to be read as one . . .

. . . about building the only kind of party worthy of the name "revolutionary" in the imperialist epoch.

• A party that's working class in program, composition, and action.

• A party that recognizes, in word and deed, the most revolutionary fact of our time:

> That working people—those the bosses and privileged layers fear as "deplorables" and "criminals"—have the power to create a different world as we organize to defend our own interests, not those of the exploiting class. That along that revolutionary course, we'll transform ourselves and awaken to our capacities—to our own worth.

Three books about building such a party. Also in Spanish and French.

Special Offer!
All three $30

The Turn to Industry and *Tribunes of the People and the Trade Unions* $20

Either book plus *Malcolm X, Black Liberation, and the Road to Workers Power* $25

CAPITALIST CRISIS AND THE FIGHT FOR WORKERS POWER

Are They Rich Because They're Smart?

Class, Privilege, and Learning under Capitalism

JACK BARNES

Exposes growing class inequalities in the US and the self-serving rationalizations of well-paid professionals who think their "brilliance" equips them to "regulate" working people, who don't know what's in their own best interest. $10. Also in Spanish, French, Farsi, and Arabic.

In Defense of the US Working Class

MARY-ALICE WATERS

Drawing on the best fighting traditions of the oppressed and exploited producers of all skin colors and national origins in the US, in 2018 tens of thousands of working people in West Virginia, Oklahoma, Florida, and other states waged victorious strikes and won restoration of voting rights to former prisoners. Those who Hillary Clinton calls "deplorables" have begun to fight back. $7. Also in Spanish, French, Farsi, and Greek.

Is Socialist Revolution in the US Possible?

A Necessary Debate among Working People

MARY-ALICE WATERS

Fighting for a society only working people can create, it is our own capacities we will discover. And along that course we will answer the question posed here with a resounding "Yes." Possible but not inevitable. That depends on us. $7. Also in Spanish, French, and Farsi.

The Jewish Question

A Marxist Interpretation

ABRAM LEON

Why is Jew-hatred still raising its ugly head? What are its class roots—from antiquity through feudalism, to capitalism's rise and current crises? Why is there no solution under capitalism without revolutionary struggles that transform working people as we fight to transform our world? The author, Abram Leon, was killed in the Nazi gas chambers. This 2020 edition has an improved translation, new introduction, and 40 pages of illustrations and maps. $17. Also in Spanish and French.

The Transitional Program for Socialist Revolution

LEON TROTSKY

The Socialist Workers Party program, drafted by Trotsky in 1938, still guides the SWP and communists the world over. The party "uncompromisingly gives battle to all political groupings tied to the apron strings of the bourgeoisie. Its task—the abolition of capitalism's domination. Its aim—socialism. Its method—the proletarian revolution." $17. Also in Farsi.

Malcolm X Talks to Young People

"The young generation of whites, Blacks, browns, whatever else—you're living at a time of revolution," said Malcolm in 1964. "And I for one will join with anyone, I don't care what color you are, as long as you want to change this miserable condition that exists on this earth." Four talks and an interview in the last months of Malcolm's life. $12. Also in Spanish, French, Farsi, Greek.

ALSO BY KARL MARX & FREDERICK ENGELS

The Communist Manifesto

KARL MARX AND
FREDERICK ENGELS

Communism, say the founding
leaders of the revolutionary workers
movement, is not a set of ideas or
preconceived "principles" but workers'
line of march to power, springing from
a "movement going on under our very
eyes." $5. Also in Spanish, French, Farsi,
and Arabic.

Socialism: Utopian and Scientific

FREDERICK ENGELS

"To make men the masters of their own form of social organization—to
make them free—is the mission of the modern proletariat," writes
Engels. The task is "to impart to the working class a knowledge of the
historical conditions and meaning of this momentous act." A classic
guide to the operations of capitalism and struggles of the working class.
$10. Also in Farsi.

Capital

KARL MARX

Marx explains the workings of the capitalist
system and how it produces the insoluble
contradictions that breed class struggle. He
demonstrates the inevitability of the fight for the
revolutionary transformation of society into one
ruled for the first time by the producing majority:
the working class.

Three volumes, $18 each.

The Origin of the Family, Private Property, and the State

FREDERICK ENGELS

How the emergence of class-divided society gave rise to repressive state bodies and subordinate status of women that protect the property of the ruling classes and enable them to pass along wealth and privilege. Engels discusses the consequences for working people of these class institutions—from their original forms to their modern versions. $15. Also in Farsi.

Anti-Dühring and Dialectics of Nature

FREDERICK ENGELS

Anti-Dühring rebuts the dogma of a reformist professor, whose backers, Engels says, sought "to spread this doctrine in a popular form among workers" and turn the working-class party in Germany into a "little sect." Bolshevik leader V.I. Lenin called it "a handbook for every class-conscious worker" aiming to uproot exploitation and oppression.

A companion work, *Dialectics of Nature,* explains the interconnection between natural science and the evolution of human society.

Both are in Marx and Engels *Collected Works,* vol. 25, $35.

The Civil War in the United States

KARL MARX AND FREDERICK ENGELS

Articles by the founding leaders of the communist workers movement on the Second American Revolution—which they followed closely as it unfolded—and why the overthrow of the slavocracy and abolition of slavery were in the interests of working people worldwide. $14

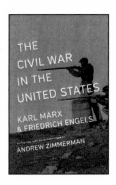

'THE HISTORY OF EXISTING SOCIETY IS THE HISTORY OF CLASS STRUGGLES'

America's Revolutionary Heritage

Marxist Essays

GEORGE NOVACK

A materialist explanation of the American Revolution, Civil War and Radical Reconstruction, genocide against the Indians, rise of American imperialism, first wave of the fight for women's rights, and more. $23

Woman's Evolution

From Matriarchal Clan to Patriarchal Family

EVELYN REED

An expedition from prehistory to class society that reveals women's still largely unknown contributions to the development of civilization. By pinpointing the historical factors that led to the subordination of women as a sex, Reed offers fresh insights on the struggle against women's oppression and for the liberation of humanity. $25. Also in Farsi and Indonesian.

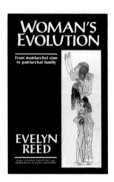

Understanding History

Marxist Essays

GEORGE NOVACK

How did capitalism arise? Why and when did this exploitative system exhaust its once revolutionary role? Why is revolutionary change fundamental to human progress? $15

ALSO FROM PATHFINDER

The Teamster Series
FARRELL DOBBS

"The principal lesson from the Teamster experience is not that, under an adverse relationship of forces, the workers can be overcome, but that, with proper leadership, they can overcome." —*Farrell Dobbs*

Four books on the strikes, organizing drives, and political campaigns that transformed the Teamsters across the Midwest in the 1930s into a militant industrial union movement. Written by the general organizer of these Teamster battles and leader of the Socialist Workers Party.

$16 each, series $50. Also in Spanish. *Teamster Rebellion* is available in French, Farsi, and Greek.

Playa Girón/Bay of Pigs
Washington's First Military Defeat in the Americas
FIDEL CASTRO, JOSÉ RAMÓN FERNÁNDEZ

In fewer than 72 hours of combat in April 1961, Cuba's revolutionary armed forces defeated a US-organized invasion by 1,500 mercenaries. In the process, the Cuban people set an example for workers, farmers, and youth the world over that with political consciousness, class solidarity, courage, and revolutionary leadership, we can stand up to enormous might and seemingly insurmountable odds—and win. $17. Also in Spanish.

Cosmetics, Fashions, and the Exploitation of Women
JOSEPH HANSEN, EVELYN REED, MARY-ALICE WATERS

How big business reinforces women's second-class status and uses it to rake in profits. Where does women's oppression come from? How has the entry of millions of women into the workforce strengthened the battle for emancipation, still to be won? $12. Also in Spanish, Farsi, and Greek.

FURTHER READING

The Clintons' Anti-Working-Class Record
Why Washington Fears Working People

JACK BARNES

What working people need to know about the profit-driven course of Democrats and Republicans alike over the last three decades. And the political awakening of workers seeking to understand and resist the capitalist rulers' assaults. $10. Also in Spanish, French, Farsi, and Greek.

Problems of Women's Liberation

EVELYN REED

Explores the social and economic roots of women's oppression from prehistoric society to modern capitalism and points the road forward to emancipation. $12. Also in Farsi, Arabic, and Greek.

Labor's Giant Step
The First Twenty Years of the CIO: 1936-55

ART PREIS

The story of the explosive labor struggles and political battles in the 1930s that built the industrial unions. And how those unions became the vanguard of a mass social movement that began transforming US society. $27

Red Zone

Cuba and the Battle against Ebola
in West Africa

ENRIQUE UBIETA GÓMEZ

When three African countries were hit in 2014–15
by the largest Ebola epidemic on record, Cuba's
revolutionary government responded to an
international call and sent what no other country
even pretended to provide: more than 250 volunteer
doctors, nurses, and other medical workers. This
firsthand account of their actions shows the kind of men and women only a
socialist revolution can produce. $17. Also in Spanish and French.

Revolutionary Continuity

Marxist Leadership in the United States

The Early Years, 1848–1917; Birth of the Communist Movement, 1918–1922

FARRELL DOBBS

"Successive generations of proletarian revolutionists have participated
in the movements of the working class and its allies. . . . Marxists today
owe them not only homage for their deeds. We also have a duty to learn
what they did wrong as well as right so their errors are not repeated."
—*Farrell Dobbs*. Two volumes, $17 each.

In Defense of Land and Labor

"Capitalist production develops by simultaneously
undermining the original sources of all wealth—
the soil and the worker." —*Karl Marx, 1867*

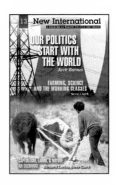

THREE ARTICLES

IN *NEW INTERNATIONAL* NO. 13
• **Our Politics Start with the World**
  JACK BARNES
• **Farming, Science, and the Working Classes**
  STEVE CLARK

IN *NEW INTERNATIONAL* NO. 14
• **The Stewardship of Nature Also Falls to the Working Class**
  JACK BARNES, STEVE CLARK, MARY-ALICE WATERS

$14 each issue

EXPAND YOUR REVOLUTIONARY LIBRARY

Dynamics of the Cuban Revolution
A Marxist Appreciation

JOSEPH HANSEN

How did the Cuban Revolution unfold? Why is it an "unbearable challenge" to US imperialism? Why are its lessons important to working people everywhere?

In "Cuba—The acid test: A reply to ultraleft sectarians," one of more than 20 articles here, Hansen starts with facts—not doctrine pretending to be theory—to examine the class struggle unfolding in Cuba in the 1960s. He refutes the political blindness of leftists who denied the dialectical richness of the socialist revolution and communist leadership developing before their eyes. $23

Lenin's Final Fight
Speeches and Writings, 1922–23

V.I. LENIN

In 1922 and 1923, V.I. Lenin, central leader of the world's first socialist revolution, waged what was to be his last political battle—one that was lost following his death. At stake was whether that revolution, and the international communist movement it led, would remain on the revolutionary proletarian course that brought workers and peasants to power in October 1917. $17. Also in Spanish, Farsi, and Greek.

Thomas Sankara Speaks
The Burkina Faso Revolution, 1983–87

Under Sankara's guidance, Burkina Faso's revolutionary government led peasants, workers, women, and youth to expand literacy; to sink wells, plant trees, erect housing; to combat women's oppression; to carry out land reform; to join others worldwide to free themselves from the imperialist yoke. $20. Also in French.